# DOLLARS AND SENSE:

## A Christian Guide to Financial Planning

**Dr. Mervin E. Thompson**

Library of Congress Catalog Card Number

Thompson, Mervin E., 1941

ISBN 0-933173164

*Printed in the United States of America*

# Table Of Contents

# INTRODUCTION

Financial planning is for each of us. Everyone in our society who makes a dollar or spends a dollar is immediately a part of our economic system. Common sense demands that each of us find the best possible way to use our money, consistent with the values and goals which we have adopted.

Money as a medium of exchange is rather simple, while most discussion of economics is complex. What most of us look for is some very basic information about the important financial decisions we face. What we get oftentimes is a document fit for graduate level consumption.

Insider language baffles and confuses us, and so we do what any good American would do, we procrastinate. Someday we will do something about financial planning, someday we will get our affairs in order, someday we will take the necessary time to sort out the maze of issues. Someday!

Christians have long struggled with ambiguity about the earning and spending of money. Should the Christian life be austere and ascetic, or should we be in the hunt like most of the rest of the world? Which Biblical picture should we endorse? The rich young ruler who is commanded by Jesus to sell all he has and give to the poor, or the faithful steward who doubles his money and is commended by Jesus with the words, "Well done, good and faithful servant."

Much of what is written today about financial planning is written for the sophisticated investor. This book purposes to cut through much of the complexity that is present, and address the major issues that each of us face. At the same time, we will be consistently conscious that we are a part of the Christian community, and that our values influence and direct everything we do, including our use of money.

Simple, and hopefully clear, introductions will be given regarding a variety of subjects. The book is intended for the average person, and certainly does not give a complete overview of all financial planning options. For more detailed information, other resources should be pursued.

A special thanks to all of the readers of the drafts of this document for their incisive and professional comments. These include Jackie Thompson, Paul Gilje, Phil Novisky, and Rev. Mark Thompson, as well as attorneys Howard Knutson and Elizabeth Holt. My assistant, Mary Jeanne Benson, provided invaluable help in proofreading and preparing the final manuscript.

Grateful acknowledgment also should be given to Lutheran Brotherhood for providing the impetus for this effort, and for absorbing the printing costs. Special appreciation goes to Vicky Obenshain, Rick Ruckdashel, Cathy Holmberg and Mark Anderson.

# A PLACE TO START

We begin with the conviction that a Christian lifestyle is our ultimate goal. Those of us who are a part of the body of Christ want to live the kind of life that God wants us to live.

Yet we are not always sure what the shape of this Christian lifestyle should be. At times we perceive that we are managing our lives rather well, our priorities and values seem to be well in balance. At other times, we seem to be off course, especially when the economic storms blow freely through our lives. So we wonder, how can we find that Christian lifestyle?

We need a place to start. Most likely this is not where we end up, but we need a place to begin. We want that place to both be consistent with Biblical teachings and yet somehow have a practical application in the particular setting where we must live our lives.

Contrasting messages seem to bombard our lives. On the one hand, we hear that money and Christian faith have nothing at all to do with each other. Most information about financial planning comes from a completely secular point of view. We can only guess how God fits into this whole picture.

On the other hand, we hear many voices today, led by the television evangelists who tell us that the Christian life is directed by a series of laws. Four or five or ten laws, to be a Christian means living in obedience to these laws. If we do not live as these media stars suggest, then we are not Christians.

This booklet rejects both of these approaches. We believe that God owns all that we have, that we are stewards of everything. At the same time we affirm that *there is no one Christian lifestyle* regarding the use of money, no one blueprint for our lives laid out somewhere that we must follow. God calls each of us to respond in our own way, out of freedom, as we are touched and guided and moved by the Holy Spirit. All of life is under the Lordship of Christ, but lifestyles of Christians vary greatly.

We offer a place to start. The concept is very simple, one which most Lutherans can follow. Obviously, there are some who do not have the financial resources to respond. But for most Lutherans, for those who have a regular income and who wish to respond to God as the owner, and who wish to pursue a Christian lifestyle, we suggest a place to begin.

## 10-10-80

Not more numbers! 10-10-80. Sounds like a credit card number, although after what we shall say about credit cards later in the booklet, be assured it is not that. Perhaps it is the birth date for a child, which it very well could be. But for us, it provides a beginning, a place to start. 10-10-80. Three parts to the puzzle.

### Give 10%    Save 10%    Live on 80%

This doesn't sound too complicated. Certainly there is nothing radically new about the formula. A Christian lifestyle could be much different from this. Yet for those who wish to have a place to start, a strong desire to respond to God's overwhelming grace and love, here is a beginning point. 10-10-80.

When a discussion about giving 10% takes place, the first question often asked is whether this comes out of gross or net income. Once again, no law exists about how we should respond, the Christian lifestyle is one of freedom and personal response. Either gross or net is perfectly consistent as a beginning point.

So many different circumstances confront people today that each one of us must work out a lifestyle as God leads us. Gross income certainly is more encompassing, take-home pay is not always indicative of one's true income. But we begin where we are, where God leads us.

### Give 10%

The Bible calls this kind of giving "a tithe". A long tradition undergirds us at this point. The people of God have responded in like manner as far back as the earliest times in the Old Testament. Giving 10% or more has been central to the Judeo-Christian faith. Jesus and the Apostle Paul strongly affirm the tithe.

Two Biblical verses highlight this kind of giving.

Malachi 4:10, "'Bring the whole tithe into the storehouse, that there may be food in my house. Test me in this,' says the Lord Almighty, 'and see if I will not throw open the floodgates of heaven and pour out so much blessing that you will not have room enough for it.'"

2 Corinthians 9:6, "Remember this: Whoever sows sparingly will also reap sparingly, and whoever sows generously will also reap generously. Each

should give what he has decided in his heart to give, not reluctantly or under compulsion, for God loves a cheerful giver."

Some basic Biblical principles lead us to respond by giving 10%.

-- God owns everything. Glen Holmquist, a former official in the Lutheran Church, tells about a conversation more than forty years ago that changed his life. Someone said to him, "Glen, you don't own anything. When do you write your check to the Owner?" Ever since, he has very diligently and gladly written the first check to the Owner, 10%, and has been a forceful advocate for the 10-10-80 lifestyle.

-- We are only given a few years to manage what belongs to God. When we leave this earth, nothing goes with us. No U-haul trailers are hitched behind hearses. Therefore, we do not hold on tightly to what we manage, or hoard what is entrusted to us; rather, we find ways to give it back to the Owner.

-- We are going against the grain. Our world seems to be caught up in an orgy of greed, we want more and more and more. Giving 10% challenges the modern creed, reminding us of the Owner and that the first check belongs to Him.

-- Giving 10% is not the end of giving, but the beginning. Most likely, the more we experience the joy and blessings of giving, the more we will want to give. How that giving will increase depends on so many unknown factors: income, health, needs of our children, occupational success, etc. No one Christian lifestyle is mandated. Giving 10% is only a place to begin.

Imagine for a moment what could happen if Christians in our nation would give 10% or more. Present estimates are that American Christian families now give well under 2%. Biblical giving could change the entire nation, as well as deeply impact the world.

If 10-10-80 became the norm, congregations could become mission centers rather than just churches. Huge sums of money could be unleashed to address world hunger, the homeless, missions and evangelical outreach. Just imagine! Think about how much could be done if Christians would start with 10-10-80. A place to begin.

Save 10%

No Biblical directive tells us to save 10%, but this idea is certainly consistent with the many teachings about debt and the responsible use of money. In some sense, saving 10% may be more radical for us than giving 10%. American habits seem to be moving in quite the opposite direction.

Saving 10% would have many important implications:

-- We would find that we are much more in control of our own financial situation. Pressures are strong in our society to spend more than we earn, to live on the edge of the cliff. Saving 10% would be a very clear sign that we indeed have our financial resources well in hand, which would give us a strong level of comfort when the storms blow in on us.

-- We would be earning interest instead of spending it. When we are borrowing money, the cost of that money is very expensive. For instance, if we borrow money at 10% interest, rather than saving money at 10% interest, that is a 20% turnaround. Spending our money on interest is not usually a very productive use of our funds, but earning interest and watching it compound is wise indeed.

-- We would be prepared for most of the crises which might come our way. A Christian is certainly not immune from the various shocks of life. The loss of a job, a depressed economy, a serious illness, a family breakup and a whole host of other contingencies can cause us financial upheaval. Saving 10% provides a cushion when the crisis comes. Expecting the unexpected is always prudent.

Just imagine what would happen if Americans would consistently save 10%, or more. Our entire economic system would be dramatically changed, for the better. Interest rates would go down, as would the alarming number of bankruptcies. As a nation, as well as individually, we would begin to live within our means.

However, the greatest benefit would come to the individual family, who would gain a measure of control which is not presently possible. Saving 10% would not only prepare us for emergencies, but also for a much more enjoyable and productive retirement. Begin by saving 10%.

## Live on 80%

A wonderful passage in the Sermon on the Mount in Matthew 6 sets the stage for us.

Jesus teaches, "Therefore I tell you, do not worry about your life, what you will eat or drink; or about your body, what you will wear. Is not life more important than food, and the body more important than clothes? Look at the birds of the air; they do not sow or reap or store away in barns, and yet your heavenly Father feeds them. Are you not much more valuable than they? Who of you by worrying can add a single hour to his life?

And why do you worry about clothes? See how the lilies of the field grow. They do not labor or spin. Yet I tell you that not even Solomon in all his splendor was dressed like one of these. If that is how God clothes the grass of the field, which is here today and tomorrow is thrown into the fire, will he not much more clothe you, O you of little faith?

So do not worry, saying, 'What shall we eat?' or 'What shall we drink?' or 'What shall we wear?' *But seek first his kingdom and his righteousness, and all these things will be given to you as well."*

It sounds almost impossible. Living on 80%, giving up much of our worry and anxiety. But it can be done. Many Christian families in our midst model this lifestyle. 10-10-80. This is certainly not where we might end up, but we are given an opportunity for a dramatic new beginning.

God also owns the 80%. We may be tempted to believe that if we give 10%, and save 10%, then the rest of the money is just for us, to be used any way we please. Not so. If God is the owner, that means the rest of our financial decisions are also under such Lordship, done prayerfully and under the guidance of the Holy Spirit. Generous giving and consistent saving does not give us license to be wasteful with the other 80%.

The balance of this booklet will deal with 10-10-80. We will look at most areas of financial decision making from a Christian point of view. Much more complexity is always possible when dealing with finances. The goal of this effort is to translate much of the technical language into simple English. Financial planning is for everyone, thus the purpose of this booklet.

# CREATING A FINANCIAL PLAN

A popular cliche asserts, "If we fail to plan, we plan to fail." More precisely, unless we are intentional about our financial decisions, unless we set our course in a specific direction, we may just spend a lifetime drifting. If we do not know where we want to go, then just about any path will lead us there.

Christians have sometimes resisted the need to plan. Such a need has seemed to indicate a lack of faith or a lack of confidence in the promises of God. Yet those reaching this conclusion misread the Biblical message. God has given us gifts and talents in order to use them, not to bury them in the ground.

Short–range and long–range planning is taking seriously God's gift of wisdom and also his directive to us to be good stewards of whatever we are given. Planning for the present and the future is essential.

## We Are The Best Planners

Many of us would rather defer to someone else in the area of financial planning. Bring on the expert! Find someone who can tell us what to do and take us off the hook. We see articles about families such as the Rockefellers who have numerous employees taking care of financial details for members of the family, and we sigh with envy.

Most of us want so much to believe totally in someone else, to give up control of our own finances. Hardly a day goes by when we do not read about yet another rich or famous person who has lost a fortune because of putting too much trust in a so–called "financial expert."

We are our own best planner. No one else has our own interests at heart like we do. No one else understands our values, principles and needs as we do. No one else is able to devote the kind of priority attention and consistent energy toward our financial future as we are.

Most importantly, no one else has to live with the results of our planning as we do. We are the best planner, number one, and whatever success we may enjoy will not happen without our full involvement, leadership and attention.

The good news today is that democracy is very much evident in the financial sector. Just about all of the information and opportunities which are available to the very rich are also accessible to the rest of us. Just about all of the high yields or the creative new products are available also to us, even if we have very modest means. With some basic education we are the best planner we can find.


## Planning Is a Family Affair

Quite often in a marriage one of the spouses becomes the "designated financial planner". The route for arriving at such a decision takes many different twists, but sooner or later one spouse usually is in charge. Most, if not all, financial decisions are made by this person. The other spouse has minimal or even no contact whatsoever with any economic matters, other than writing checks.

However, resulting emotions in this arrangement may not be minimal, because each of us attaches different meaning to money and approaches it differently.

Financial planning should be done together. In a marriage, a wife and husband should work as a team, cooperating to make all the major financial decisions. When only one person is involved, resentments inevitably grow. The planner can resent having to do this alone, the non planner can resent being left outside of the process.

A large percentage of family conflicts revolve around the use of money. How much money a family receives is not usually the issue, rather the ownership or lack thereof causes the problems. Consistent communication between spouses would do much to bring them closer together, as well as giving them a common purpose and direction in the marriage.

Popular writer Charlie Shedd once said that he and his wife Martha have a very specific way of making major decisions. They pray together about the particular issue, then they pray separately. If after praying through the situation they both come to the same conclusion, they then believe that this is God's will for them. If they do not agree, they go back to praying until they can find some common ground.

If married couples would pray together, plan together, live together under the guidance of the Holy Spirit, much would be changed. Both wives and husbands should take seriously the role of financial planning, so that they can help set the tone and the direction for their life together.

## Singles

Single persons represent the fastest growing segment of American society. Many of them are single parents. Although the family situation is different, one element of financial planning is quite similar.

Planning together with another person concerning financial matters is usually better than planning alone. Far better to gather with a parent, a brother or sister, a son or daughter or a valued friend than to try to chart a course in isolation. Support and affirmation and encouragement are important ingredients of financial planning.

## Setting Family Goals

We begin our planning process by setting goals. Each family will need to do this on its own, no ultimate blueprint covers all of us. Each member of the family should have input and responsibility for planning. Goals should center around a number of different areas.

— Spiritual goals: growing in Biblical knowledge, experience of faith, and living a Christian lifestyle.

— Family goals: strengthening relationships, spending more time together, planning vacations, showing acts of love.

— Work–related goals: continuing education, career planning.

— Personal goals: working towards maintaining health and wholeness, physical fitness, relationships with others, friendships.

— Service goals, serving in the community, the church, participating in certain causes and movements.

— Financial goals.

The purpose of this booklet is to help think through and make decisions about financial goals. Write your goals on paper. Studies have shown that those who write out their goals are much more likely to achieve them. In the following chapters, we will examine the most pressing issues for that planning process.

# WHERE TO LOOK FOR A FINANCIAL EXPERT

As mentioned in the previous chapter, we are the best financial planners. We may not know the difference between a mutual fund or a CD, but we have the most to lose and the most to gain. We must be a part of the planning process.

However, there are times when we need help. We can walk only so far into the forest, when suddenly we realize we don't know precisely where we are. The time has come for a guide who can help us find a compass to discover the right path to our goal.

Where do we turn? How can we find someone who combines both the financial expertise as well as a sense of value and integrity? Plenty of good news and bad news surrounds our search.

<u>Good News About Experts</u>

-- Oftentimes such a person can see much more clearly where we are headed with our present plans than we can. A mid-course correction is all that is needed to keep us on the right path.

-- A planner can often give us affirmation when we are right on track. Fear and uncertainty often plague the average person as we venture into the financial arena, but a person in the know can give us much needed confidence and support.

-- A planner can be a sounding board for some of the most important decisions we will ever make. Decisions about money are often done in secret, away from any feedback or dialogue. But as we share basic goals and strategy with one other person, just talking them through will bring a sense of perspective and new insight.

-- A planner can draw upon some resources that are normally unavailable to us. The rapid advance of technology and computerized services can open new doors to our efforts. New software is continually being developed which can be most helpful in our planning.

-- A planner can provide us with basic information that would be difficult and time-consuming for us to find on our own. The financial arena changes almost daily, and a good planner will be up-to-date and keep us from making any decisions based on outdated information.

## Bad News About Experts

-- Planners very often have no understanding or appreciation of Christian values and goals. Charitable giving holds no real interest for them, thus the lack of expertise here. Not only do we not receive encouragement or sage advice about percentage giving, but sometimes the planner even seeks to dissuade. Giving for tax reasons seems to be the only motivation to give.

For instance, in the September, 1988 issue of Good Housekeeping, several planners combine to give advice to a selected family. This family has chosen out of strong Christian convictions to give 15% of its income each year as a commitment to a local congregation. When the church had a building campaign in 1985 and 1986, the family contributed nearly 25% of its income. Obviously the church is the central focus of this family's life.

When the financial planners analyze this budget, it is clear that they are most uncomfortable with the level of giving which is present. Thus, the consensus opinion reflected in the article is that the family should substantially reduce its giving, and thus realize other financial goals. Giving is depreciated, other values are more important to the planners.

-- Financial planning is a huge growth industry. An estimated 150,000 planners now are looking for clients. Some are very skilled, and some are inept, with many somewhere in between. Unfortunately, no national standards are required, no specific educational background expected. Just about anyone can claim to be a financial planner. Buyer beware!

-- Planners often come primarily as salespersons. Products which bring the planner maximum financial return are strongly promoted, regardless of what the needs might be. Planning is not necessarily connected with purchasing.

-- Planners who work for a fee may put together the most beautiful plan in the world, but if the proper products are not found to go with the plan, it doesn't mean much. Much higher costs can also accompany such expertise, no matter what the quality might be.

-- Specialists are more common than generalists. Because of the complexity of the financial markets, planners have expertise in increasingly narrow categories. This often forces us to find several advisors, driving up the price.

Planners are both good news and bad news. Our task is to know the difference and to find someone who can bring us information we need. Some guidelines for choosing are as follows:

## Choosing a Financial Planner

-- Before such a selection, we should be very clear about our own values and the basic direction of our lives. When we have already made the decision of 10-10-80, then it is time to find the help we need. Require the planner to fit into your value system, not the other way around.

-- Find a planner who gives ample evidence of a Christian commitment. We want someone who understands and affirms our values and lifestyle. Perhaps this is someone from our own Lutheran church or some other church in the community, someone who is well respected as a Christian living out his or her faith.

-- Choose a planner who has expertise in the area of charitable giving. A person who has been a strong giver over the years will most likely have gained a good deal of expertise in this whole arena. Ask many questions at the outset about a commitment of the planner to giving. Ask about tithing. Probe the subject in depth to discover the level of expertise.

-- If the planner works for a company, research how active that company has been in the charitable giving field. Many companies have spent substantial resources in developing new ideas in the charitable giving field. We want someone as a guide who can call on the whole range of charitable giving options.

-- Find a planner who will most likely be around in the future, as well as the company represented. Too many people have put their trust in planners who are just passing through the territory, here one day and gone the next. We want connectedness over the long term.

-- If the planner has products to sell, make sure that these stand up against the best in the field. Check *Consumers Report*, check the yields in various publications. A one per-cent interest difference over a long period of time can make a significant difference. Minimize the up-front costs, find the best return over the long run. Comparison shop.

We are the best planners. At times we need the help of an expert. Choose that person with much care. When recommendations are made that are puzzling, get a second opinion. Don't put all of your trust in any person, only God deserves that response. We need to find someone who we like, who we trust, who has integrity and Christian values. Then we are on our way to sound financial planning.

# THE FOUNDATION OF ALL FINANCIAL PLANNING, A BUDGET

Without a budget, we are adrift. Without a carefully planned and systematically followed budget, we are floundering around in the white water without a paddle. To decide where we are going and how we are going to get there necessitates a budget. Some observations:

— It is easier not to develop one. That may not be surprising news. The path of least resistance is to let the chips fall where they may. It is also the most frustrating. Budgeting takes a very conscious decision, a commitment.

— Once a budget is planned, the implementation is not all that difficult. A couple of hours a week is usually more than enough time to carry out the paper work, to itemize everything that we spend. Working a plan is mostly common sense and consistency.

— A budget brings self discipline into our spending. What it means is that we sometimes have to say no to an immediate want. But this action is much easier when we have a plan. We always will have limited funds chasing unlimited places to spend, but budgeting keeps this in balance.

— A budget gives us the wonderful sense that we are in control of our finances. Being out of control is a very defeating and debilitating way to live. A budget frees us by following the plan we have created.

— A budget is not some form of punishment, some treatment for those who cannot seem to get a handle on their finances. A budget is for everyone, a systematic, sensible way of setting and reaching our financial goals.

The following is a sample of a cash flow system, which can be adapted to fit any individual or family. *

Step 1 — Monthly Income Summary
    Salary
    Part-time
    Interest
    Dividends
    Other
   * Personal Cash Management System, Lutheran Brotherhood.

The total monthly income should be deposited into your primary checking account. A master record of this account should be left at home. An interest-bearing checking account is preferable.

## Step 2 — Giving 10% or More

Once we have received our total income, we now determine what our giving will be, based on a percentage of what we receive. Write the first check or checks to the Owner.

Local Congregation, weekly giving
Local Congregation, special gifts
World Hunger
World Missions
Community Needs
Other

## Step 3 — Saving 10% or More

The next check goes to our own future. We should decide on investment goals, the specific places, and then pay the money into these accounts.

Life Insurance
Money Market
Savings Account
Mutual Fund
Stocks
Bonds
Land or Rental Property

## Step 4 — Deferred Expense Savings

Some expenses do not occur monthly, but less frequently. Included in this category would be real estate taxes and homeowners insurance (unless these are escrowed), auto insurance, vacation funds and major purchases. Spread the impact of these purchases over a longer period of time, so the monthly cash flow will not be disrupted.

Real Estate Taxes
Income Tax Not Withheld
Auto Insurance
Homeowners Insurance
Major Purchases
Vacation
Gifts, such as Christmas, birthdays, etc.
Major Home Improvements

## Step 5 — Monthly Fixed Expenses

These generally permit very little control, because they are paying for necessities. We must keep the form current, changing the numbers as our situation changes.

Mortgage or Rent
Electricity, Heating Costs
Telephone
Water and Garbage
Auto Loan
Health Insurance
Child Care

## Step 6 — Variable Expense Summary

Once the first five steps are completed, we can then figure out how much money is available for variable expenses. We cannot spend more than we have allocated, the limits are clear. We need accurate records in our master account at home, so that we know how we are doing at all times.

If credit cards are used, deduct and circle the amount of any purchases from the checking account at the time of purchase, so no surprises come back to haunt future cash flow.

Gasoline
Auto Maintenance
Food
Clothing
Medical and Dental
Drugs and Medicine
Gifts
Personal Care
Home Maintenance
Education
Newspapers and Magazines
Recreation
Entertainment
Cash
Children's Expense
Other

We have tried just about everything else. Perhaps now is the right time for us to try a budget. We have nothing to lose except our financial chaos.

# THE NEED TO GIVE

Giving 10%. We do this not because God so much needs our money, but because we need to give. In response to what God in Jesus Christ has done for us – loved us, died for us, made us his children – we are motivated to give far more than what the world sees as reasonable. Giving becomes a passion in our lives, a major reason for living.

The Biblical promise says that giving will bring blessings and joy. The more we give, the more we rejoice. Whether we are wealthy or stewards of very few possessions, the directive is the same. It is more blessed to give than to receive. God loves a cheerful giver.

Two different kinds of giving challenge each of us. First, we plan to give. When we plan ahead, we are able to give far more than we would otherwise give. By setting some specific giving goals, by praying for the resources we need to fulfill those goals, we can often stretch our giving substantially.

For instance, if we wish to give a generous gift in the future, we can prepare for that in the present. By setting aside any discretionary income, by postponing some purchases which are not entirely necessary, or by increasing our income or cash flow, we can prepare. Or if credit cards are causing us to spend more than is prudent, we can put them away for a time—perhaps never finding them again. Planning to give often increases the amount we can give.

A second way to give is spontaneously. Many needs arise on the spur of the moment, and we do not want to be so locked into a plan that we cannot respond. Special appeals in our local congregation, a crisis in the world, a serious accident of someone in the community can each lead us to want to give a generous gift. Be flexible enough to respond whenever the need might be present.

Ways To Give — Giving Now

Obviously, the most common form of giving is that which we do out of our current income. When we give 10% of our income away, we are giving now. That giving goes to our local Lutheran congregation, which very much depends on our giving for its ministry.

We also contribute to a wide variety of special appeals — world hunger, mission work, local food and clothes closets, United Way, church colleges, camps and institutions.

In addition, we want to be able to respond to the major drives which come our way. If our local congregation may be having a building program, this is a time to give much more than we normally give. A church college, the YMCA, the local orchestra are having a fund drive for a building or endowment, and we want to give a substantial gift. Our gift most likely will come out of current income or savings, or it might involve a gift of property.

A favorite way of giving in recent years is that of a gift of stock, particularly one which has appreciated in value. Many benefits come to the giver in addition to the joy of being able to give. What is particularly appealing is that all of the capital gains taxes which would normally have to be paid are eliminated, and the donor receives a deduction for the appreciated value. Such a deal!

Gifts of other property are also common. New tax rules now govern the giving of such gifts.

### Property Worth Less than $500

The donor needs to receive a signed receipt from the charity with a clear description of the property, plus date and name of organization. The donor estimates the value.

### Property Worth Between $500 and $5000

The above information applies here as well. In addition, we need a written record of how and when we acquired the property and its cost. In addition, tax form 8283 must be attached to our Form 1040.

### Property Worth More than $5000

Major changes have taken place for these large gifts. A reputable appraiser must be hired to assess value, one who had nothing to do with the original purchase nor with the disposition of it. The work must be done within a time period of 60 days prior to the date of the gift and the date of the filing of the tax return on which the gift is reported.

In addition, the appraiser must sign IRS form 8283. Without this, the charitable contribution will be forfeited. Included with this form are the appraiser's qualifications, name of firm, method of evaluation that is being used and acknowledgment that the appraiser knows the work is being done for income tax purposes.

Some of the property gifts which are most advantageous to give in the present include:

| | | |
|---|---|---|
| Antiques | Art Work | Business Inventories |
| Collections | Crops | Jewelry |
| Land Contracts | Livestock | Life Insurance |
| Mortgages | Notes & Leases | Real Estate |
| Royalties | Stocks & Bonds | |

## Ways To Give Later

Life Insurance:

—Purchase a policy which designates a charity as the irrevocable owner and beneficiary. A rather modest tax deductible premium will assure a sizeable future gift.

—Change the beneficiary of an already owned policy to a charity.

—Add the name of a charity to the list of beneficiaries on an existing policy.

—When a policy is paid up, give it outright.

—Assign annual dividends from policies to a charity as a regular means of giving tax-free income.

Real Estate:

Such property can be given outright, so that the charity then owns the property. A full tax deduction is received.

Property can also be given, but the donor can continue to use the property. Called a life estate agreement, a person can give a residence or farm and continue to live there. Another option is to give real estate and continue to receive income for life. Tax benefits are substantial on such gifts.

## Ways To Give and Receive

A *trust* is a most effective way of giving and receiving. A trust is an asset given by one person to another for the benefit of a third. Sound confusing enough? A trust is taking some asset and giving it under the control of someone else, so that the property can be given to another party.

In other words, a person wants to give a gift to a church. That gift is placed in trust, under the control of a trustee. The instructions are that the gift will go to the church, but under the terms specified in the trust. Many tax benefits occur in such an effort.

Two basic kinds of trusts are available.

### A Living Trust:

Established while you are alive, it can be either revocable (which means it can be changed or revoked) or irrevocable (once established cannot be changed). Revocable trusts have fewer tax advantages.

A major advantage of a trust is that it avoids the probate process, which can be very long and involved and costly. In addition, a trust is never made public, unlike a will which goes through public probate.

Property owned by an irrevocable trust is not a part of the estate when the estate tax is figured. This means that any individual who has assets over $600,000, $1.2 million for a married couple, will pay substantial taxes. A chart of estate taxes is included.

| Taxable Assets | Estate Taxes |
| --- | --- |
| 600,000 | –0– |
| 1,000,000 | 153,000 |
| 2,500,000 | 833,000 |
| 5,000,000 | 2,083,000 |

Two irrevocable living trusts illustrate the flexibility and the desirability of such ways of giving.

Charitable Remainder Trust. The donor may place any amount of money in the trust, receive income for life, and have the remainder pass to a charity at the death of the second spouse. A large current tax deduction is also present.

Charitable Lead Trust. The donor may again place any amount in the trust, and the income from that trust can be paid to any charity for a specified number of years. At the end of this time period, the assets can either come back to the donors or their heirs. This assists the charity now and gives a large tax deduction to the donor.

On lead trusts, an income tax deduction is only available if the asset reverts to the donors. An estate tax deduction, on the other hand, is only available if the property goes to someone other than the donors.

### Testamentary Trust:

Unlike the living trust, this is created by the will, and will only take effect after the death of the grantor. While it is similar to the living trust in many ways, it does not avoid probate. However, it can direct how the assets can be distributed.

Charitable giving is at the center of the life of the Christian. Becoming aware of some creative ways to give is not a means of giving less, but giving more. If present tax law will multiply the amount of the gift, why not take full advantage of this opportunity? For more detailed information, someone with expertise in charitable giving should be consulted.

# BORROWING MADE UNEASY

Economic life in the last quarter of the 20th century can be characterized by one word, *debt*. Whether we are describing the federal government or individual consumers, the major common denominator has been that of borrowing. We are alarmingly in debt. Our nation has very rapidly been transformed from a creditor nation to a debtor nation, putting us all at risk.

Why this rush into debt? Forces of every kind have pushed us into an addiction toward borrowing. Offers of credit come to most of us every week, solicitations from banks, savings and loans, credit unions, huge corporations. The vast majority of these offers come in the form of the credit card. Borrowing is so alluring and easy, simply sign the signature card and turn the plastic loose.

What makes borrowing extremely appealing is that we can have whatever we want up front to gain immediate gratification. We can enjoy the benefits of the product before we have to pay. Miraculous. In a fast food culture, immediacy is highly valued. The tendency of past generations to wait and plan and save in order to purchase something of value is simply unacceptable for the modern person. We want everything now.

Debt has brought serious problems to many families. For one reason or another, the family has slipped over that invisible line into a place where debt has taken control. Freedom has been surrendered to the lender. The following chapter will discuss in more detail how we know when we are in trouble.

Credit Cards

Causes of debt are complex. Many reasons could be given for why we are on such a borrowing binge. Envy and greed certainly are near the top of the list. However, if there is one major factor in pushing us toward the brink, it has been the advent of the credit card. Not just one card is sufficient for most families, but a multitude of cards which fill the billfold or the purse.

Estimates today suggest that we spend up to 34% more when we are using a credit card than when we are relying on cash. Imagine, 34%! While this figure could be contested, all of the research thus far suggests that credit cards do entice us to spend a good deal more money than we would otherwise spend.

Obviously, if this is true, the best way to eliminate many of our cash flow problems would be to eliminate or sharply curtail the use of credit cards. In fact, we might even realize a dramatic increase in the amount of discretionary money we can use. Credit cards loom as a chief culprit in ushering us into the age of debt.

How do we respond? What are some constructive ways to live in this present world, and yet not become overwhelmed by the temptation to borrow our way into prosperity?

Some suggestions:

—Credit cards can be very helpful in some situations. For instance, if we are traveling, the right cards can bring us much convenience, as well as lessening our dependence upon large sums of cash. Also, a credit card can be invaluable in the case of emergency — a car breaking down or running out of necessary funds. Again, it is beneficial to make sure that the amount charged is subtracted from the checkbook, so that no surprises will come as the bills start arriving.

—Limit credit cards to just two or three, using those with the most universal acceptance. Let the rest of the cards go. Take a large scissors and do some plastic surgery, cutting the cards into little pieces.

—Comparison shop for credit cards. Institutions are pushing their cards so emphatically because they are enormously profitable. Interest rates on cards range from just over 10% to 30% or more. Annual fees can range from nothing to more than $50. Often an initial time period is free, but then the annual fees begin.

—Understand the grace period allowed on the credit card. How long is the time frame after the purchase has been made before interest is charged on the account? Many cards give from 30 to 45 days or even more. However, some other cards begin to charge interest from the day of purchase, even before the charge is posted on your account. Compare!

—Pay bills on time. If, heaven forbid, bills are paid late and interest charges are assessed, find a credit card with the lowest possible interest rate.

—If borrowing is absolutely necessary, home owners can take a close look at a possible home equity loan, rather than the credit card. Not only is the interest rate usually much less, but the interest paid is deductible from income tax.

## Questions To Ask Before Borrowing

— Is the borrowing consistent with our Christian lifestyle? Will the additional debt still allow us to give 10%, save 10% and live on 80%? Can we stay out of bondage to the lender?

— Is the borrowing consistent with the financial plan that has been prepared? Are budget guidelines being observed? If the purchase goes beyond what has been planned, where will the difference be found?

— Does the increased debt make any economic sense? In other words, does this purchased item appreciate or depreciate in value? Within this scenario, the purchase of a home would in most cases be a very wise investment, but to borrow heavily to buy a car or a major appliance would make much less sense.

— Borrowing also has some important psychological and emotional implications. In other words, can we increase our debt and still retain a comfort level in our lives? How much risk and debt can we stand, what are our limits?

Borrowing has become a way of life. Yet we need not let it overwhelm us. We should be very hesitant to assume any more debt unless it is consistent with the financial plan we have established. We should pay no more interest than is absolutely necessary. Consider the elimination of all credit cards. If we decide to use them, make them work for us, not the other way around.

Proverbs 22:7b "The borrower is servant to the lender."

# SIGNS OF FINANCIAL TROUBLE

Dr. Oswald Hoffman, well-known speaker on the Lutheran Hour for the past generation, tells the story about Gumperson's law. Most of us have heard of Murphy's law, but it is Gumperson's law that often seems to be most in touch with real life. Gumperson's law goes like this:

<u>The probability of a given eventuality is in inverse proportion to its desirability.</u>

This explains a lot of things, how you can drop a half lighted match out of the window of your car and start a forest fire, and yet not be able to light the dry logs in your fireplace with a whole box of matches and the whole Sunday edition of the newspaper.

It explains how the children can be exposed to mumps twenty times in a row and not get them, and yet get them without any exposure at all the night before the family goes on a vacation. Or how a man can buy a suit with two pair of pants and burn a hole in the coat.

Hoffman says that there is no telling how far J.P. Gumperson might have gone had it not been for his untimely death in 1947. He was walking along the road on the left side, facing the traffic the way you are supposed to, when he was hit from behind.

In some sense, Gumperson's law is alive and well in the financial dealings of our lives. Oftentimes we can also say, the probability of a given eventuality is in inverse proportion to its desirability. In other words, the very result we fear the most is sometimes exactly that which happens.

## Denial

One of the most amazing phenomena in our modern world is the number of people who have somehow managed to end up in deep financial trouble and do not seem to know it. Oblivious to all of the rather clear and unmistakable signs, they simply do not give evidence of understanding what is happening to them. For those on the outside looking in, we are baffled at such behavior.

Part of the reason for not reacting seems to be the common tendency among humankind to deny that which is too painful to accept. Death often brings a similar reaction, we refuse to believe that such an event has taken place. Denial and death often go closely together.

Financial crisis can also bring on similar forms of denial. People can be bumping up against the edge of the precipice time and again, with creditors and collection agencies lined up outside the door, and yet there often remains a pollyanna-like belief that some kind of dramatic financial windfall will bring salvation at the last moment.

Perhaps this is one reason why the golden promise of the lottery brings such a positive response, especially among those who have very meager financial resources. Hope springs eternal, and the poor are just one number away from the miracle of deliverance. Unfortunately, the lottery and other such promises are mostly cruel hoaxes, perpetrated against those people who can least afford the risk.

## How To Know We Are in Trouble

Without financial plans or goals, trouble is often hard to discover. If we do not know where we are headed, then we have trouble knowing when we have drifted off the track. The key to understanding exactly where we are is to develop a specific financial map for our present and future.

Once our plan is in place, once we are clear on our own goals and priorities, then we can know immediately if we are leaving the road and heading down a dead end. Much of the subjectivity can be eliminated, either we are following the plan we have created, or we are not. Either we are making progress, or we are sinking into difficulty.

Lending institutions have developed some specific criteria for identifying people who are moving into the danger zone. If these characteristics are similar to our own pattern of financial behavior, then financial danger is near.

—We pay only the bare minimum each month on credit and never pay more than the minimum.

—We make partial payments rather than full.

—We start falling behind on payments shortly after opening an account.

—Our account balance always seems to grow, we cannot seem to pay it off.

—We have periodic bouts of late payments.

What are some reasons why American society seems to push us toward overspending? What is it in this particular time of our history that makes it so difficult to stay within specific limits?

# Lifestyle Characteristics Which Often Lead to Trouble

—We spend more money than we are earning. Our desired lifestyle is beyond what we can afford. Our home may be more expensive that we can handle, our car payments may be far too high, the vacation we want is more than we should realistically spend. So we turn to our credit cards, and we are in trouble.

—We are not saving. Giving 10% and saving 10% are impossible. When we live on 110% of our income, to have 20% for giving and saving is just a dream. Thus, we have no cushion, no life preserver when the unexpected expenses arise.

—We have no budget. Nothing controls our spending except our own emotions, the whim of the moment. We buy something and worry about paying for it later.

—We experience a sudden or unexpected crisis. Our financial plan may have been in place, but suddenly the situation is dramatically changed. Perhaps there is the loss of a job, a reduction in income, a divorce, a death, an illness. Everything quickly unravels.

Oftentimes married couples have become completely dependent on two incomes. While this arrangement can give substantial financial freedom for many, if one of these incomes ends, crisis can follow right behind.

While this is assuredly idealistic, the most stable situation a married couple could reach is if the family could live on just one income, rather than two. A second income could then be used for *extraordinary expenses*, such as college, investments, savings, preparation for retirement, vacations, etc. The loss of one income would then certainly impact the financial goals of the family, but it would not cause the kind of crisis that is presently so common.

—Giving is limited to leftovers. When we are spending more than we are earning, when we barely have enough money to meet credit expenses, giving becomes a burden rather than a joy. Priorities have flip-flopped. Rather than giving our first check to the owner, we are giving that which is not already used up, and that most likely is minimal. God has been pushed out to the margins, rather than living at the center of life.

Financial problems do not usually come from too little financial resources. Rather, they come from misplaced priorities, by a lifestyle out of control.

Spiritually, emotionally, and psychologically we have lost our bearing, and we are in real danger of crashing. Strong and decisive action is needed. A new lifestyle is absolutely necessary. The time to begin is now.

# FINANCIAL TROUBLE DEMANDS DECISIVE ACTION

When the ship is sinking, no time for inaction exists. Analyzing can only go so far and then it becomes a paralysis of analysis. We need to dedicate our most immediate and best efforts to facing the problem, right now. In a real sense, the future depends on it.

Joseph Conrad in his novel *Typhoon* tells a dramatic story about action in the midst of trouble. A violent storm is in process in the China Sea, and a great sailing vessel is suddenly in jeopardy. In the narrative a young man named Duke is asked to take the wheel of the vessel and is given the following counsel by the captain:

"Keep her facing it. Don't be put off by anything. Keep her facing it. They may say what they like, but the heaviest seas run with the wind. Facing it, always facing. That's the way to get through. You are a young sailor, so face it. That's enough for any man. Keep a cool head and face it."

Jesus gives us a magnificent image in the 6th chapter of Mark. He has returned to his home town and has been rejected. Those people who should have accepted him, supported him and loved him have chased him out of the community. Sorrow and pain are obvious in Jesus. No one enjoys being rejected.

So he takes his disciples aside and teaches them an eternal lesson. When people reject you, he says to them, what you need to do is to shake the dust off your feet and move on. When life around you gets to be very dusty, when there seems to be no hope, shake the dust off your feet and get moving. Kick them high, shake off all of the dust of failure and heartache and launch out into a new style of life.

Several steps are necessary.

*Admit the problem.* Get rid of the denial and the self protection and take ownership of what has happened. Many very intelligent, powerful and faithful people have found themselves in deep financial crisis. Company is not hard to find at a time like this. Accept responsibility and admit the nature and scope of the problem.

Support groups are springing up all around us these days. Many of these are founded on the 12-Step program first developed by Alcoholics Anonymous. Now, however, many different groups are using the 12-Steps.

While many of the steps would be applicable to the area of finances, two shed particular insight and direction.

*First, we must admit that the financial area of our life is out of control* – Our life in a very real sense has become unmanageable. Once that step of being totally honest has been taken, then we are open to the kind of healing and change which is necessary.

*Second, we must accept the transforming power of God* – When we have finally admitted our own sense of powerlessness, we are then able to accept the power of God fully into our lives. We have tried to do everything by ourselves, but have run into one dead end after another. Now is a wonderful opportunity not only for a financial change, but for a spiritual awakening as well. Prayer becomes central as we open ourselves to God. We shake the dust off our feet and move on, with the power of the Spirit of God moving us forward.

*Avoid bankruptcy* – Relatively recent changes in the law have made it far easier to declare bankruptcy. What this has done, of course, is to enable many people to simply give their financial problems to someone else. A creditor, either an individual or an institution, is now left holding the bag for the actions of another.

Certain situations may leave us with no other option. No possibility of repayment might ever be possible. However, these situations are rare. Investigating every other alternative is essential. Bankruptcy should not be an easily acceptable action. We are responsible for our own lives, we need to own our decisions and do whatever is possible to extricate ourselves.

*Create a financial plan* – Rather major changes in our lifestyle will be demanded if we are to extricate ourselves. Expenses must be curtailed ruthlessly, and perhaps other sources of income should be sought. For a short time a second job may be appropriate, or a married household with only one income may require two.

Just as important as creating a new plan, however, is tenaciously following the guidelines. Planning is only as effective as our willingness to abide by what it says. Addressing the debt and finding ways to reduce it must be the top priority. For instance, if credit cards have contributed to this situation, then plastic surgery may be required. Rip them up or at least put them away for a time and use only cash. Desperate circumstances require strong corrective measures.

*Consult someone trustworthy for counsel* – Perhaps this is someone who does financial planning for a living, or it can be someone we know who has good financial sense. A member of our church or someone with whom we work may be good sources of help.

Even though we may tend to be lone rangers when it comes to financial planning, even though secrecy seems to be next to godliness, we must make sure to find someone who can help chart a course for the future. Honest feedback is invaluable as we seek to find our way out of the financial woods. In addition, the support and encouragement of someone whom we trust will make this a much easier journey.

*Work out a repayment schedule with creditors* – Most institutions to which money is owed are more than happy to work out a reasonable payment schedule. They want nothing more than to be paid, and if they find someone totally committed to meeting all obligations, they will most likely be very helpful.

Sometimes it is best to consolidate all debts into one place. If many of our debts are in accounts with high interest rates, such as on credit cards, by all means we must find a loan which will mean substantially lower rates. If a home equity loan is a possibility, we should wrap all loans into one of these. Not only are the interest rates lower than most other debt, but the interest paid is tax deductible.

*Commit yourself to a new long-range plan* – Short term efforts to break free from the overwhelming debt are essential, but this is not enough. Equally important is the establishment of a long range plan so that such a situation will never happen again. Losing weight is not ultimately satisfying if we just gain it all back again. Debt must never again overwhelm us.

We should consider strongly the lifestyle suggested in an earlier chapter, give 10%, save 10%, live on 80%. Borrowing should only be an option for purchasing a home, not for credit cards, not for consumer debt such as cars, furniture or vacations, not for anything which does not increase in value. Never spending more than is earned should become a guide by which we live.

*Help others in similar straits* – Often the most effective caregivers for others are those who have been through similar circumstances. Having experienced the particular pain and anxiety and humiliation by admitting that life was indeed out of control, we are uniquely prepared to be helpful to others.

Find others in your congregation who have a similar interest, and form a task force to look at ways people can be given good financial counsel.

Consider organizing support groups or seminars on money management, inviting well qualified resource people to participate in such an educational process. When we catch a vision of what needs to be done, God will give us whatever resources are necessary to do it.

# TEACHING CHILDREN ABOUT MONEY

Children may not have classes in financial planning, they may not have any formalized education in handling money, but they have already learned a great deal. By watching their parents, they have appropriated some very specific attitudes and behavior patterns.

Most of what is learned from parents is caught more than taught. What is communicated is a value system, a life style, a set of principles. Watching our children handle their money is often like looking in a mirror, and that in itself tends to make parents uncomfortable. Why do our children have to be so much like us, especially in areas where we are not all we know we should be?

Several different kinds of attitudes seem to predominate among adults, and these, it seems, are communicated most effectively to children.

*Conservative and Cautious* – Many parents who have grown up in homes where money was scarce, or where they have strong memories of having to go without, tend to be very reticent to spend money. Debt is strongly resisted, money is meant to be saved and kept for a rainy day.

Those who were raised in the depression of the 1930's are often classic examples of this kind of attitude. Pay cash for just about everything, stay out of danger, thriftiness is next to godliness. Basic to the handling of money is the admonition to be careful, to use extreme caution, cut down the risk factor. Spend only when necessary.

*Copping Out* – Some parents have decided that the handling of money is tedious and frustrating, better left to someone else. In a marriage situation, one of the partners often feels this way, giving up almost all responsibility for any financial dealings. A simple allowance is enough, let the other person take care of planning, investing, saving and spending.

Children learn from this parent very quickly that it is entirely possible to avoid the hard realities of life. Find a caretaker as a spouse, someone who will enable the other one to be irresponsible, and be freed from this chore. If something is unpleasant, ignore it, let someone else do it. Unfortunately, this contempt for financial activity can easily translate into disdain for those who have to do it, including the other spouse.

*Controlling* – Some parents attempt to control the use of every penny that the family earns or spends. A controlling attitude is not usually limited to

39

finances, but here it can be manifested in a very specific way. Nothing can be spent unless it is first approved by the controlling parent or parents.

Children in such a system soon learn to be afraid of making any independent financial decision. With constant fear of alienating the controlling parent, the ability to grow up and be responsible is diminished. A very clear power struggle may be taking place in that home situation, and the children are often caught in the middle. This is hardly the proper attitude for entry into adulthood.

*Impressing Others* – Many adults look at money as a very effective way to win friends and influence people. Lavish spending becomes a means by which others are impressed. A spirit of flashy purchases brings instant attention. The possibilities of gaining notoriety through spending are almost endless.

Children quickly learn that money can be a way of improving their own reputation, of rising above the rest of the crowd. Friendships can be bought, attention can be secured through the use of money. A life goal might be to accumulate huge sums of money, so that friendship or status might never be wanting. Ultimately, children in this system do not learn the value of money, but only perceive it as a way to impress others.

*If Attitudes Conflict* – Perhaps the most damaging atmosphere for children is one in which the two parents seriously disagree on the value or use of money. For instance, if one spouse is a controller and the other wants to impress friends and neighbors, conflict is inevitable. If one spouse is a controlling personality and the other chooses to cop out, a form of dictatorship is established and communicated.

Children need to experience some real consistency regarding the way money is valued and spent in the family. Even though husbands and wives come out of very different backgrounds and experiences, working together on a financial plan and sticking to that plan will communicate a strong unity to the children. Children are adept at finding cracks in the parents' relationship and using those areas for their own use. A unified front from the parents which is well conceived and consistent is the best approach.

How are we doing as parents? In a recent survey, only one-fourth of teenagers responding said that their parents have provided a positive example to be followed in the area of finances. Less than 30% have encouraged their children to do any saving at all. Such inattention has borne some bitter fruit.

We will find numerous benefits to our family if we become more intentional about communicating money priorities. We simply cannot hope that they will develop proper attitudes if all they can rely on are scraps that might fall from the parent's table. Some suggestions for this teaching include:

## Bring Money Decisions Out Of The Closet

For some reason, secrecy and intrigue have marked much of people's attitudes about money. Finances have had this mysterious quality, talked about in hushed tones behind closed doors, late at night. Enlightened parents as we are, we have begun to talk more openly about sex, death and other difficult issues, but money often seems to be the last taboo.

Why not share with our children how much our income will be, and how we are planning on spending that money? Why not ask for input from our children on how the money should be spent, discuss values and priorities and goals. Let them know that money is limited, that making choices always involves saying yes and also no. The more open the discussion becomes, the less mystery that is involved. The less mystery, the less power money is given over us.

## Communicate Your Christian Values About Money

What a significant opportunity we have to teach our children about a Christian lifestyle. Often we try to communicate with children about faith and life, but such things are so abstract. Issues such as trust and hope and love and peace are hard to communicate. This is why Jesus told so many stories. In the concreteness of the story we understand more fully the abstract truth.

Not much is abstract when it comes to money. Here we can talk about how God owns it all, and we are giving 10% of our income back to God and saving 10% for the future. Children can see, through our own decisions about money, just what priority our belief system carries. No wonder many adults who are among the leading givers in congregations learned about giving at their parents' knee.

## Provide A Regular Allowance For Children

Some parents claim that no allowance is needed, the parent will supply every need. Yet there remains no better substitute in learning how to handle money than by actually doing it. Children need to wrestle with financial decisions, to experience the pain and pleasure of saving over a period of time for something they dearly want. In addition, they need to discover the consequences of spending too much, and having to go without for a time. It is best to learn these lessons when the stakes are relatively small.

Right from the beginning children should be taught how to give and to save. However, in that amount they are permitted to spend, they should be given a great deal of freedom. Parents can find it instructive to give up the desire to control every decision. Instead, they can let the child learn the lessons which need to be learned.

Ron and Judy Blue in their book, *Money Matters for Parents,* suggest that as children get older, they have five different envelopes in which to place their money — one for giving, one for saving, one for gifts, one for clothing, and one for spending. The children are free to move money back and forth from three of these envelopes, but not from giving or saving.

## Children Need To Learn Relationship Between Work and Money

Many jobs around the house should not, of course, earn money. These are done simply because the child is a part of the family. But other specific jobs which are deemed to be over and above the routine may have some kind of financial "reward" associated with them.

Giving our children an opportunity to work and to earn a reasonable amount is sound preparation for adulthood. A list of income earning opportunities might be developed, and a child can begin to see the relationship between labor and reward.

## Consider a Clothing Allowance

In our modern day world, probably no area of financial spending is more difficult and volatile than that of clothing. Pressure is exerted by every clothing ad we see on television or in magazines. As in the purchase of a car, such decisions involve status, ego, and peer response. To buy basic clothing would be easy, to deal with the emotional and psychological implications is much more complex.

Planning a clothing allowance at the beginning of a year and then giving a child a certain amount of money each month can greatly lessen the pressure. Parents then are not under duress to constantly buy clothing items that become the latest fad. In addition, if a child with an allowance chooses to spend large sums of money on designer footwear or jeans, the lesson is quickly learned that very little remains for anything else. The sooner a child learns that funds are limited and difficult choices are a part of life, the better off we all will be.

Teaching children about money is primarily done by involving them in our own goal setting, our own discussions of values and priorities. As children discover why we do what we do, what it means to live as stewards of what God has given to us, they will understand much more clearly the meaning of money. The best time to begin this communication would be yesterday, but since that is past, why not begin today?

# HOME SWEET HOME

Home ownership has been at the center of the American dream for a majority of families down through the years. Not everyone has shared in that dream, of course, yet the dream is still alive and well. Tax policy by the federal and state governments has not only encouraged such a purchase, but has made it exceptionally attractive as an investment.

While shoveling snow, mowing lawns and painting this and fixing that may not be especially alluring to many, benefits of home ownership usually do outweigh the drawbacks.

<u>Incentives for Home Ownership</u>

— Appreciation of Value. Even though the inflationary spiral of the 1970's has waned in most sections of the country, homes are still increasing in value. Unless the area is especially depressed, there is every reason to expect that a home will be worth more in the future than today.

— Taxes on Appreciation. Remarkably, we do not have to pay any tax on money which is earned in the home until the property is sold, and perhaps not even then. After selling one home, if a more expensive home is purchased within two years no tax is paid. What this offers is an excellent way to grow assets without having taxes take a significant portion.

— Tax Benefits of Purchase. Many tax advantages are available to the home buyer. Most settlement costs are fully deductible. Interest costs on the mortgage as well as real estate taxes can provide huge tax breaks. Tax changes in 1986 eliminated many opportunities for tax reduction, but basically left untouched those associated with home ownership

— Home Equity Loan. Whenever borrowing becomes necessary, such as financing the purchase of a car, a vacation, medical bills, or funding college expenses, a home equity loan is the best place to turn. Such a loan must be repaid, and the original price of the home plus the cost of improvements imposes a ceiling on what can be deducted. Yet all interest on home equity loans is deductible, while interest paid on consumer loans will be gone after 1990.

— Retirement Nest Egg. After reaching the age of 55, a new tax law takes effect called the 55 Rule. When a home is sold by someone who is 55 years or above, as much as $125,000 in profit can be pocketed tax free.

Given that the owner has lived in the house for three of the past five years, and that both husband and wife agree to this decision, the *55 Rule* can provide a wonderful tax–free nest egg.

—Estate Foundation. Most likely the equity in a home will be the largest single asset in the estate that is left to our heirs. Money will derive from either the sale of the home after the death, or it will come from the cash received when the home was sold and invested over a period of time.

## A Second Home

Just about everything that has been said about the purchase of a home can also be said of the purchase of a second home, such as a vacation residence. Large tax deductions are available because of interest and real estate taxes, and if the home appreciates in value, it can provide a valuable asset for the estate. The 55 rule would not apply on a second home.

A word of caution is in order. Americans are oftentimes overloaded with busy schedules. Married couples, often both involved in careers, are pressured on the one side by extensive demands from work and on the other by that substantial chunk of time required to maintain a home. Most often the upkeep of a home is labor intensive, involving a rather large commitment.

What we often do in order to get away from the pressure and the intensity of life is to purchase a second home by a lake, in the country, or by a mountain. While this sounds like the perfect solution, especially with the tax benefits, the results may be less than perfect.

In essence, what happens is that we work incredibly hard during the week, then pack the car for the weekend, drive a distance to a vacation home, and spend the weekend repairing or maintaining a second house and yard. For some this is truly the way to relax, but for many a change in scene at the vacation "home" simply spells more work. A second home needs to be thought through very carefully, for it may be much more than a sound investment.

## How Much Home Can We Afford?

As indicated above, decisions about buying a home are not only economic, but also psychological and emotional. How much debt can we comfortably absorb into our budget? How much risk can we handle? If we sense that the cost of the mortgage is more than we can afford, most likely we should not buy that home.

In other words, can we still retain our basic values and priorities while purchasing the new home? Are we able to continue to give 10% and save 10% and still meet all of the obligations of this new home? If we have to turn our back on all of our present obligations and commitments in order to take this tremendous leap, then we might be paying too much.

Arriving at a ballpark figure on what the average family can afford to pay is quite subjective. However, some lenders have settled on what is called the *28-36 rule*. In essence, the total expense of the home — interest, principal, insurance and taxes — should total no more than 28% of the gross family income.

In addition, when the home expenses are added to any other long-term debts, with ten or more monthly payments still outstanding, such as car or student loans, all of this cannot total more than 36% of gross family income.

Other factors can play a part in this formula. If less than 10% is put down on the home, this formula may be reduced. On the other hand, if a good credit history is present, if a substantial down payment is pledged, or if liquid assets are available which equal at least three months of the house payments, the guidelines can move upward.

A survey completed in 1987 found that fewer than one third of those who planned to buy homes planned to spend more than 25% of pre-tax household income on housing. Therefore, a rule of thumb should be considered: *25% of the family gross income is getting very close to the limit of what can be afforded for a home.*

Mortgage Loans

Rest assured that the new home is not the largest purchase we will ever make, rather it is the mortgage which claims the top prize. Mortgage costs can often double or triple the actual cost of the home, or more. Certainly, ample tax benefits ease the interest costs, but paying more interest than is absolutely necessary is still not cost effective.

Some ways to reduce long-term costs for a home are as follows:

*30–Year Mortgage* – One distinct advantage of the longest possible mortgage is that less money is tied up in the investment. For those who do not plan to stay in the home over the entire life of the loan, minimum payments might be advantageous. This would enable extra money to be invested somewhere else. Because of the much higher interest costs on the longer mortgage, most of the payments would be toward interest and thus provide tax deductions.

*15–Year Mortgage* – More than half of the interest costs can be saved by reducing a 30 year loan to 15 years. In addition, the interest rate will normally be lower, from 1/4 to 1/2%. Monthly payments will be somewhat higher, but not nearly as high as might be expected.

*Reducing Principal* – Whether we have committed ourselves to a 30-year or 15-year mortgage, interest costs can still be reduced by paying a few more dollars each month than is due. Amounts can vary from month to month, but the results are a reduction of principal, and ultimately, of interest.

*New Options* – Providing home mortgages is a fast-changing industry. New products are emerging every year. Some lenders are now offering either 10-year or 20-year loans in addition to those more common in the industry.

*Bi-Weekly Mortgage* – Paying on the mortgage every two weeks rather than twice a month is another possibility. What happens is that 13 full payments are made each year instead of 12. Surprisingly enough, this will shorten the payoff date from 30 years down to 18 or 19, saving substantial interest.

*Adjustable Rate Mortgages (ARM)* – Rates on these loans run approximately three percentage points lower than the 30 year fixed mortgages. Adjustments are made periodically based on the prevailing cost of money at that time.

ARMs are especially attractive for those who plan to pay a mortgage in a relatively short period of time, or who anticipate a steady rise of income in the future, to cover any rise of interest. Such mortgages pay off extremely well if interest rates hold steady or decrease.

Crucial to an ARM is the adjustment cap. Interest rates should not be allowed to rise or fall more than 2 points at each adjustment. A maximum of five or six points over the life of the mortgage should be a total cap. Otherwise, the costs to the borrower can be highly prohibitive.

*Convertible ARMs* – Ability to convert adjustable rate mortgages to fixed rate has been quite limited in the past. However, new flexibility has become more common. Some lenders now allow a borrower to convert to a fixed rate anytime during the first three years of the loan, or anytime between the first and the fifth years. Predictions are that this option will spread.

*Consulting an Attorney* – Bringing an attorney into the home buying decision early can save considerable dollars. Quite often a buyer signs a purchase agreement and then brings it to an attorney for review. However, at that time it is too late to change many of the basic commitments of that agreement. Consulting an attorney before signing the purchase agreement would be a wiser course.

*Computing a Loan* – Finding ballpark figures for a loan involves only a relatively inexpensive calculator, but for those who still work by pencil, here are some tables based on a cost per thousand for the loan. To find the monthly payment, multiply the dollar amount by the following numbers.

| Length of Mortgage | 9 1/2% | 10% | 10 1/2% | 11% |
|---|---|---|---|---|
| 15 Years | 10.44 | 10.75 | 11.05 | 11.37 |
| 20 Years | 9.33 | 9.66 | 9.99 | 10.33 |
| 25 Years | 8.74 | 9.09 | 9.45 | 9.81 |
| 30 Years | 8.41 | 8.78 | 9.15 | 9.53 |

For example, to calculate the payment on a $75,000 mortgage financed for 15 years at 10% interest, multiply 75 by 10.75 to get a monthly payment of $806.25.

Buying a home remains the single best investment for most people. In addition, the tax implications are substantial. While many other factors enter into the decision, financially speaking, such a purchase makes excellent sense.

# BUYING A CAR

Home buying may be quite subjective, but at least there are some basic guidelines to consider. We look at how much mortgage debt we can assume, the various tax advantages, the needs of our family, the investment benefits. Purchasing a car, however, transports us to an entirely different realm.

Covering basic transportation needs is relatively easy. Low-cost options are readily available, either in the new car or used car arenas. If our basic goal is to keep car expenses as a minimal part of our budget, we could accomplish this without too much effort.

However, buying a car is not usually confined to the realm of finding basic transportation. It quickly becomes clear that emotions and self image are also involved. An argument between the head and the heart is common, and the heart has a way of prevailing. Budget busting decisions take place in the car showroom perhaps more often than anywhere else.

Not only are the adults of a family participating in this decision, but the children as well. Common to many parents is the experience of having a child get wind of a proposed purchase of a car that is cost effective, and in effect vetoing that decision. Rather than a grey station wagon with four cylinders, the family ends up with a red convertible and the fanciest stereo system made.

According to advertising, a car is more than a car, more than transportation. A car is meant to give us whatever we might lack. If we are short on sex appeal, the purchase of a certain model of car will suddenly give it to us. If we want charisma, a particular car is the answer. If we want status among our neighbors, the car dealer has just the right deal waiting for us.

Most of us are intellectually aware of how absurd these claims are, yet we all to a degree are influenced by them. Much more is spent on a car or cars than we would deem to be reasonable or necessary, or even affordable. How can we be more intentional in spending less, in following our budget, in avoiding the great American love affair with the automobile?

Some Observations:

—In most situations, the least expensive car to drive is the one we already own. Unless the car is unable to function effectively anymore, or has become dangerous to drive, that vehicle already paid for is the cheapest transportation we can find.

—Purchasing a car with cash is without a doubt the most effective way to proceed, unless the interest rates on a loan are at very low levels. Setting aside the money in advance would not only earn interest during the time of saving, but also save double digit interest costs on the loan.

—If borrowing for a car is the only alternative, the most cost effective loan is the one secured by your home equity. Not only are the interest rates lower than most car loans, but these costs can be deductible.

—Haste makes waste. When searching for a car, set aside sufficient time. Salespersons often exert pressure by asserting that any purchase later than ten minutes from now will most likely cost you more and provide you with much less selection. Not true! Comparison shop, find the prices and selections at several different places before deciding.

—What makes buying a car so much different from many other financial purchases, as well as quite unappealing to many, is that the price is meant to be negotiable. It is often easier to buy something if the price is set, and that is it. But we know that bargaining is expected, and many of us do not like this kind of game playing. In addition, it seems as if the dealer is holding all the cards, and we are rather helpless in the proceeding.

Quite the contrary. We must decide how much we are willing to pay for a certain car, including all extras and taxes, and then make an offer. We must be prepared to walk away if the price is not met, and leave a phone number in case the offer sounds more attractive to the salesperson later in the day. Attraction for a certain car should never take away our power in these negotiations.

Used Cars

Finding a used car in excellent condition can help us avoid the high price of driving a car off the showroom floor. At the same time, risks are always present in such a purchase. We may be buying someone else's lemon. Some things to consider when looking for a used car:

—Determine in advance how much money can be offered for a particular car. Discipline is required once the decision has been made, since the temptation to "move up" is strong.

—Research what is on the market, taking sufficient time and care. Certain publications list the markup for every model of car. Knowing this information helps in negotiations with a seller. Public libraries and bookstores have good resources for determining approximate value of a certain model of car.

— Watch for cars in your neighborhood which are for sale, or those in the want ads sold by individuals. This will give some indication of the approximate worth. In addition, during certain times of the year car sales may be especially slow, giving the buyer an opportunity for a better price. If the buyer will keep the car for a relatively long period of time, buying that car in the beginning, middle or end of the model year will not make much difference.

— When a car appears to be the right one, before purchasing consider the following questions. By far the best course to take would be to contact the previous owner.

Is the mileage correct?
How many owners has the car had?
Has the car ever been in a serious car accident?
Has the car been used to tow a large boat or trailer?
Why is the car being sold?
Are records available for maintenance work?

— When all of the questions have been answered, a mechanic should be secured to check the car very thoroughly. A clean bill of health from a trusted mechanic is essential. In addition, make sure that the title and a written bill of sale signed by both parties are a part of the transaction.

Several states have a Used Car Warranty Law, which requires licensed dealers to provide written warranties on used motor vehicles less than eight years old, having less than 75,000 miles on the odometer, and selling for $3,000 or less.

The Minnesota law requires an expressed warranty for at least 60 days or 2,500 miles, whichever comes first, on used vehicles with less than 36,000 miles. For those with more than 36,000 and less than 75,000, the warranty is effective for a minimum of 30 days or 1,000 miles.

New Car Warranties

Longer warranties on new cars have become much more common recently. Some include up to 7 years or 70,000 miles on the powertrain, which consists of the engine, transmission and other machinery which moves the car. A warranty may even be offered of up to 7 years and 100,000 miles on body rust.

Unfortunately, as consumer advocates point out, good warranties in the areas of the car which usually break or wear out are still not common.

Car dealers often want to sell a customer a *service contract*. The cost is usually from $300 to $800 to extend the basic warranty on certain parts for an extra one to six years. In most cases, a wiser course is banking the money and earning interest.

Three warranties should be examined before purchase.

—Basic warranty. Several cars now have extended the terms to air conditioning, brakes, suspension, steering and electrical system for an extra two to five years. This is an excellent improvement in the coverage.

—Powertrain warranty. A key question has to do with how much is charged when the car is brought in for service after the first year is over. Many dealers charge $100 each time.

—Corrosion warranty. Many manufacturers require that rust burn a hole completely through the metal before the warranty is honored. Surface rust will not be covered after one year regardless of coverage.

How to Maximize a Warranty

—Save receipts for required maintenance to back up any claims for repairs under warranty, as well as to demand free repairs in case problems develop after coverage ends.

—Assume all defects are covered. When in doubt, ask the dealer or the manufacturer's regional or zone office.

Buying or Leasing?

In most cases, purchasing a car with cash, or for home owners, borrowing from a home equity loan is the most economical way to proceed, unless interest rates on the loan are well below market averages. Lease agreements may mean a lower monthly payment, but the big difference is that at the conclusion of the lease, the car still belongs to the dealer.

Leasing is especially attractive in conserving the dollars that are necessary up front, and the lower monthly payment can free up more cash flow. Also, the cost and hassle which accompany trading a car can be eliminated. What is rather surprising today is to see all of the leases advertised which also call for a down payment, flying in the face of one of the strongest reasons to lease in the first place.

Costs for leasing are less because the full cost of the car is never paid, somewhere between 33% and 50% remains when the car is returned. However, a car in reasonably good condition will cover the terms of the lease.

Leasing does not necessarily simplify the challenge of car shopping. Spending the necessary time researching the various options and looking at the many different cars as well as lease arrangements will most likely be as time-consuming and difficult as before. Leasing does not lessen the need to check all possibilities thoroughly.

### Two Basic Kinds of Leases

—Closed End Lease. This is without a doubt the most popular form of lease, sometimes called a walk away lease because the car may just be turned in when the lease ends. Assuming the car has been properly maintained and the mileage limits have not been exceeded, the value of the car in the marketplace is of no concern to the one who has done the leasing. Bring the car to the dealer and then walk away.

—Open End Lease. A guaranteed price for the leased car is no longer assured when the lease is completed. If for some reason the car is worth less than expected, the leaseholder must make up the difference. Experience shows that most consumers are not willing to take that risk, so there are far fewer of these leases.

*Mileage limits* — A leased car can generally be driven from 12,000 to 18,000 miles a year without penalty. Anything more than the limit will bring an additional charge of 6 to 12 cents a mile. For those who are likely to drive more than the limit, negotiating a higher monthly rate on the lease agreement in the beginning is wise. Money will be saved by this approach.

*Length of Lease* — Much variety is present in the term of leases, but as is true with purchased cars, the trend is definitely toward longer leases. With customers looking for the lowest possible monthly payments, 48-month to 60-month leases are not at all uncommon.

Lower monthly payments should not pressure the lessee into agreeing to a term longer than the time the car is wanted. Ending the lease early will bring a very high price. For instance, breaking a 48-month lease after just 24 months, one half of the way through, will be re-figured as if a two-year lease was chosen in the first place. High costs are assured.

In summary, purchasing or leasing a car is a subjective decision. The uncertainty or difficulty of such a decision can be greatly diminished by planning ahead and knowing the approximate amount of money to be spent. Comparison shopping can give far more assurance that the money which is allocated for an automobile is well spent.

# HOW TO PAY FOR COLLEGE

Do we wake up in the middle of the night in a state of utter terror? Do we enroll our precocious little child in some specialized computer class before diapers have been outgrown? Do we get up way before dawn to transport our six-year-old to some kind of athletic extravaganza?

Such silliness must mean that we are afflicted with a common malady, worry about paying our children's college costs. We have been carried away with the staggering predictions being bandied about and have panicked. We sense there must be a more reasonable and sensible way to prepare for college than trying to raise an Einstein or a Mary Lou Retton, but so far that remedy has escaped us.

Before we lose all sense of perspective and rationality, we need to be assured that we can take some steps to prepare for that most challenging moment. By pursuing some very common sense strategy, we can do a great deal to ready ourselves for that first shocking college bill. Of course, there are no guarantees that we will have enough money for the entire amount, depending on where our children decide to go to school, but some good advance planning will help immeasurably.

Some suggestions:

— Begin to prepare now. Today is the right time to begin, no matter what the age of our child. Granted, if the child is just short of 18, the options are much more limited than if the child is age 7, but begin now. How much we set aside may not be as important as the regularity and continuity of such preparation. To attempt to fund college costs out of normal family cash flow is a luxury only a few can afford.

— Do not put all hopes in the possibility of scholarships. Various kinds of scholarships and gifts may indeed be offered, but most of these are based on need. Especially gifted students in academics or athletics or music certainly can be awarded wonderful scholarships, but the numbers are relatively few.

For every superstar who might walk away with a $16,000 a year military scholarship or earn a prestigious merit scholarship, a whole chorus of students who also have excellent talent and potential will have to fund college entirely on their own.

If by chance our child is one of the chosen few who is coveted and eventually recruited and financed by a particular college or university, rest assured that we will be able to find other worthwhile places to use the money we have so diligently saved for college. However, we should not count on such a gift, the percentages are not in our favor.

—Realize that colleges and universities are trying to soften the blow of college payments, so they have dramatically increased the amount of financial aid as the cost of tuition has risen. Most but not all of that aid is reserved for families who have very limited financial resources. Many parents have had the experience of filling out numerous financial aid forms, taking rather large blocks of time in such efforts, and then being summarily turned down for all aid. For the middle income wage earner, most of the cost of college will be borne by the family.

—For those who do not have sufficient funds for college costs, numerous loan programs are available. The best of these has been the *Guaranteed Student Loan program* (GSL), now called the Stafford Student Loan (SSL). Prior to 1986 no needs test was applied to families with incomes under $30,000, however that has now changed, thus eliminating many families who previously could have benefited.

For those who qualify, by all means consider the SSL. New limits as of 1986 are $2625 for years one and two of college, and $4,000 for year three, four, or, if necessary, five. Graduate students can also borrow up to $7,500 a year. Counting loans for both undergraduate and graduate school, an undergraduate can borrow as much as $17,250 and a graduate student $54,750.

No money need be paid while the student is in school. Repayment will not begin until six months after college is completed. The interest rate is 8% for the first four years of repayment, 10% thereafter. Because of the 1986 tax law, interest will no longer be deductible after 1990.

Numerous other loan opportunities are available. Two examples are the PLUS (Parent Loans for Undergraduate Students) and the SLS (Supplemental Loans for Students). These are supplemental loans which are not based on need, and are available above and beyond the SSL. The interest rate is somewhat higher than the SSL and is variable; however, it will never exceed 12%.

The borrower is responsible for the interest throughout the life of the loan and repayment begins in 60 days. However, there are several deferment options which allow the borrower to defer payment of principal and, in some cases, interest during the in–school period. Students can borrow up to $4,000 per year.

Once again, the *home equity loan* is a very effective way to finance college costs. Not only is the interest rate generally lower than most other loans, but the interest costs will continue to be tax deductible.

How to Prepare for College Costs:

Gifts

When a child is born, one of the first acts of the parents should be to secure a Social Security number, and to start an account under the Uniform Transfers to Minors Act (in some states called the Uniform Gift to Minors Act). Begin to channel funds into that account right from the beginning, and let it be known to others that this college fund is already established.

An advantage of such an account can also be a disadvantage. When established in the child's name, the parents will never be able to use this money in the case of an emergency. In most cases, however, this will be beneficial. The fund will never be looked upon as a source for funding other needs.

The tax bill of 1986 changed the playing field. A child under the age of 14 can only earn up to $1,000 in interest or dividend payments and still be taxed at a low rate. Anything more than $1,000 will be taxed at the parent's rate, although that is certainly quite a bit of income. At age 14, the limitation ends. Then a child can earn up to $3,000 of all kinds of income without paying any tax. Changes continue to be made in the tax law; therefore, it is prudent to check federal, state and local ordinances before making these decisions.

Compounding

Compounding is the key to saving for college. Relatively small amounts invested early in a child's life can grow to rather sizeable amounts over a period of fifteen or more years. Systematic, disciplined giving to a college fund will bear much fruit, more than we might imagine.

For example, depositing $100 a month for 18 years at an average return of 12% would total $75,786. A return of 12% may sound out of reach, but many mutual funds have had returns far in excess of that amount over a period of years.

The most secure way to save is through a Certificate of Deposit (CD) or through a Savings Bond, for instance a U.S. Government 'EE'. Bonds are exempt from state and federal taxes until the bonds are redeemed or mature. Maturing now in 12 years, they are especially appropriate for parents who have young children. Bonds purchased recently and held at least five years have a guaranteed minimum rate of 6% and a current variable rate of 7.17%.

An example of how savings for college compounds is as follows, as well as an indication of how higher interest rates can multiply the returns. $1,000 a year is set aside each year in this table.

|         | 6%    | 7%    | 8%    | 9%    | 10%   |
|---------|-------|-------|-------|-------|-------|
| Year 1  | 1060  | 1070  | 1080  | 1090  | 1100  |
| Year 2  | 2184  | 2215  | 2246  | 2278  | 2310  |
| Year 3  | 3375  | 3440  | 3506  | 3573  | 3641  |
| Year 4  | 4637  | 4751  | 4867  | 4985  | 5105  |
| Year 5  | 5975  | 6153  | 6336  | 6523  | 6716  |
| Year 6  | 7394  | 7654  | 7923  | 8200  | 8487  |
| Year 7  | 8897  | 9260  | 9637  | 10028 | 10436 |
| Year 8  | 10491 | 10978 | 11488 | 12021 | 12579 |
| Year 9  | 12181 | 12816 | 13487 | 14193 | 14937 |
| Year 10 | 13972 | 14784 | 15645 | 16560 | 17531 |
| Year 11 | 15870 | 16888 | 17977 | 19141 | 20384 |
| Year 12 | 17882 | 19141 | 20495 | 21953 | 23523 |
| Year 13 | 20015 | 21550 | 23215 | 25019 | 26975 |
| Year 14 | 22276 | 24129 | 26152 | 28361 | 30772 |
| Year 15 | 24673 | 26888 | 29324 | 32003 | 34950 |
| Year 16 | 27213 | 29840 | 32750 | 35974 | 39545 |
| Year 17 | 29906 | 32999 | 36450 | 40301 | 44599 |
| Year 18 | 32760 | 36379 | 40446 | 45018 | 50159 |

Mutual Funds

An investment which raises the risk level a bit is the purchase of shares in a mutual fund. One advantage of such an investment is that both dividends and capital gains can be automatically reinvested over the years, increasing the compounding potential. Also, no taxes are paid until the funds are withdrawn. Average returns over past years have been higher than that of CD's or Savings Bonds, but more risk is present as well.

To reiterate, once money is given to a child in a Uniform Gift to Minors account, parents cannot reclaim it. If a young person at the age of eighteen chooses to buy a Porsche rather than use the money for a college degree, parents have no legal way to stop it. For more control over the money, some other investment vehicle should be chosen.

## Single Premium Whole Life Insurance

Surviving the tax bill of 1986 was an excellent investment opportunity in life insurance. For a lump sum amount, for instance $5,000, we can purchase a life insurance policy. Coverage should be on the parent's life, not the child's. The wage earner should be protected.

Yield on the money will vary depending on the prevailing interest rates and what investments will be purchased with the premium. All gain is completely sheltered from federal income tax.

When our child reaches college age, we can then borrow from the cash value of the life insurance policy, keeping only about a 15% remainder. We should never take out all of the cash value or cancel the policy, for that would require income tax to be paid on every dollar received. Leave the 15% to heirs. Congress is in the process of taking another look at this tax sheltered income, so watch closely the decisions made in Washington.

## Work Income

For those who have any kind of personal business, no matter how small, children can be hired as employees. No age limit is set on this employment. Children can be paid a fair wage for just about any kind of work, which is deducted from the business and put into an account for college. Documentation of such work is most important, with hours and job descriptions included.

Businesses which are not incorporated need not pay any Social Security taxes on the wages. Children can earn up to $3,000 a year without paying any income tax.

## Zero Coupon Bonds

These bonds may be purchased for almost any amount of money and then be redeemed many years later at a much higher value. For instance, they could be purchased to mature at the very time a child is entering college. Yield on these bonds is determined by the interest rate at the time of the purchase and is locked in until the day of maturity.

Interest on zero coupon bonds is usually taxed, although tax is deferred on some bonds. However, interest rates are lower on tax deferred bonds.

## Trusts

Placing assets in a trust at one time was an effective way of saving for college, in which the income of the trust was taxed at the lower tax rate of the child. The new tax law changed the rule. If a trust was established before March 1, 1986, hang on to the trust, the tax advantages of these older trusts are retroactive. But do not add any more money to the trust, this would mean that the trust would lose its tax advantage.

<u>Grandparents</u>

A potential resource for helping with college costs or any future education costs for our children are grandparents. Obviously, this is not true for everyone, but for many it is a place to look. Many times grandparents are at peak earning power when their grandchildren are born. At the same time they have finished paying college costs and other expenses of raising children.

For many grandparents, putting $1,000 or $2,000 aside in a college fund for a grandchild would require very little effort. This gift could either be on a recurring basis each year, or it could be in a different form, such as a single premium life insurance policy. Grandparents should not only think about giving to heirs in their will, but also when the money might be even more needed.

<u>For More Information</u>

Write for *College Money Guides, 1989-1990*. Included are twelve different publications which can give specific help in finding the money for college. Send to this address:

> Octameron Associates
> P.O. Box 3437
> Alexandria, Virginia 22302

Write for *The Student Guide—Five Federal Financial Aid Programs*, a 60-page booklet explaining eligibility requirements and application procedures for Pell Grants, Perkins Loans, Guaranteed Student Loans and others. Send to this address:

> U.S. Department of Education
> Training and Dissemination Office
> 400 Maryland Ave. S.W.
> Washington, D.C. 20202

# INSURING THE PRESENT AND FUTURE

Imagine living in a perfect world. Disease and accidents and premature death no longer happen. Homes are never robbed and automobiles never crash. Everyone lives happily ever after. Such descriptions sound almost heavenly.

Yet all of us are painfully aware that we inhabit no such world. Danger and uncertainty accompany us every step of the way. At just about the time we believe our life has become rhapsodic and trouble-free, something upsetting rains on our parade. Tragedy and heartache and the possibility of financial reversal are never far away.

Insurance is a vehicle our society has created to give at least some sense of security and preparedness in this often chaotic world. We cannot insure our future beyond this life, only God can do that, but we can give our families some degree of comfort if some mishap would come our way.

Paying the costs of insurance may seem to many of us a rather unproductive way of spending our hard earned income. However, we have no choice, we need to be adequately insured on a variety of fronts and therefore prepared for any eventuality that might take place. Insurance coverage takes many different forms.

## LIFE INSURANCE

At first glance, such a product seems to provide primarily death insurance. If we die, particularly earlier than expected, our family in some sense wins. If we live beyond the normal life span, in terms of insurance, we lose. Such a characterization was especially true in the past, where the actual return on a life insurance policy was so low.

Recent years have brought dramatic changes in the life insurance industry. Because of the longer life expectancy of Americans, premiums have appreciably dropped in price. In addition, investment opportunities have been greatly improved, centering in higher interest rates as well as cash value.

One single key which makes life insurance such a valuable investment today is the ability to borrow from the policy, tax free. A low rate of interest is charged on the loan, but repayment is not necessary. Not repaying the loan, of course, will mean decreased value of the policy at the time of death.

Life insurance can be purchased in many different ways. Some policies incorporate a type of *variable* dimension. Variable means the buyer may choose to have the premiums invested in a variety of different options, and often has the freedom to move those funds around as the market changes. A comparison can be made with a savings account vs. a mutual fund. Variable life insurance, like a mutual fund, carries more risk, but also has the possibility of higher future cash value.

By way of comparison, the annual premium for an average whole life policy of $100,000 for a non-smoking male has been about $1,300, although today there is substantial premium flexibility. Since women live so much longer than men, the cost of a policy for a non-smoking female who is age 35 is approximately 20% less than that of a man.

<u>Universal Life</u>

In recent years, many alternatives to traditional whole life insurance have been created. One of the most popular is that of Universal Life. Basic to such a policy is a flexible premium schedule. More money can be paid when the interest rates paid on investments are higher, less can be submitted when cash flow may be short. Beyond a minimum, how much is paid is left up to the buyer.

Interest rates are higher than on whole life policies, and premiums are significantly lower. Estimates of the minimal annual premium for a $100,000 policy for a 35-year-old non-smoking male can be one half of what it might be for whole life.

Sales charges for life insurance usually are taken from the very beginning, up to 50% of the first year premium and 5% thereafter may be eaten up. Make sure to comparison shop, measuring the sales charge in relation to the rate of return. These are long-term decisions. Universal life insurance should be held at least ten years, so that the investment can repay the money already spent on commission and fees.

We also must make sure that we have enough accumulated cash value to cover the monthly deductions for death protection and policy expenses, when we choose to pay less in premiums. The company is required to inform us when we might be getting close to this situation.

## Term Insurance

Term insurance is, without a doubt, the least expensive kind of life insurance protection for younger persons. A healthy 35-year-old non-smoking male can buy $1 million of term insurance for less than $1,000 a year. Basically this is death protection, no cash value or investment possibility is a part of this policy.

Most common among the various alternatives is *Annual Renewable Term.* As long as the premiums are paid, the policy can be renewed year after year. However, as the policy holder grows older, the rates for this insurance climb. Until the age of 40 the rise is only a few cents per $1,000, but beyond the age of 40 it can accelerate quite rapidly.

*Decreasing Term* is the other major form of term insurance. Under this plan the premiums which are paid stay the same year after year, but the benefits decrease with advancing age. Where such a policy can be especially appropriate is in insuring a declining debt, such as a home mortgage.

A level amount for a term policy can also be arranged, which means that a person is paying a higher cost in the earlier years and a lower cost in the later years.

Many term policies are *convertible*, which gives the owner the option to switch to whole life or universal life without a new medical examination. In addition, some policies may provide a way to apply some term premiums already paid to the new policy.

## Disability Insurance

For many, this form of insurance is at least as valuable as life insurance. While it may be almost impossible for us to conceive of an illness or accident which would prohibit us from working for several months or even longer, a survey by the Social Security Administration indicates that 6% of Americans are classified as disabled.

When considering disability insurance, we look first of all to our employer. Many benefit programs already include disability coverage; other plans offer this possibility. However, if the group policy at the place of employment has insufficient benefits, separate policies can be purchased in order to supplement present coverage. We also need to be aware that benefits from a group policy are taxable.

Private disability plans cover up to 60% of work income, but no more. Two reasons are given for this apparent shortfall. First, the benefits are not taxable, so less income is needed. Secondly, the employer and insurance company want to encourage the employee to return to work, so all income is not replaced.

Premiums for disability insurance vary widely, depending on the nature of our work. For those who work in a relatively safe environment, premiums will tend to be a good deal lower. For those who do sky diving or clean windows on skyscrapers or perform other more dangerous work, premiums will no doubt be significantly higher.

Blackout Period

When purchasing the various kinds of insurance, we need to be aware of the times in our lives when we are most vulnerable. Chief among these for most people is that time after the last child leaves the nest until the date of retirement. For most couples this is somewhere between ten or twenty years. Some reasons for the vulnerability are:

—Social Security benefits are very limited during this time; not until the age of 62 do they have full value.

—Most couples plan on doing the majority of their saving for retirement during these years. If one spouse is gone all of this changes.

—Pension plans are usually paid on the highest salary years. An early death or disability would greatly lower the overall potential for those benefits.

—Inflation over a long period will make any fixed income increasingly inadequate.

Wisdom dictates that we purchase the insurance we need for each period of our lives. During the years of age 25-45, we need most of all to insure family income. After age 65, our greatest need is asset replacement. The years between 45 and 65 offer the greatest opportunity to save and also present us with our greatest vulnerability.

Insurance coverage should be considered with the blackout period in mind. During years where risk is the greatest, appropriate coverage should be in place. Wise planning up front can save enormous heartaches later on.

## HOMEOWNERS INSURANCE

Compared to other forms of insurance such as health, car and life, homeowners insurance is relatively inexpensive. However, coverage of a home and its contents is no less important, and in most cases a home mortgage cannot be secured until an adequate policy is in place. Again, comparison shopping is a must. Some guidelines:

—Homes should be insured for at least the replacement value, the amount that would be required to replace the house. 80% of the market value is a rule of thumb. Remember the land will not burn.

—Contents of the home should also be insured for replacement value. Traditionally, homeowner policies have insured possessions for one half of the value of the home, but for many families that is inadequate. By increasing a premium about 15%, contents can be insured for replacement value, rather than depreciated value.

—Generally a deductible of $250 is reasonable, anything less than this amount becomes quite expensive. Raising the deductible to a higher amount, for instance $1,000, can make a significant reduction in the premium.

—Extra insurance should be purchased for high value items, antiques, art work, baseball cards, stamp collections, family heirlooms, jewelry, etc.

—Liability coverage in the past has been in the range of $100,000, but that is no longer enough. At least $300,000 should be considered, possibly more.

Often an umbrella policy can be purchased which will cover liability on both house and car. $1,000,000 is a recommended amount, at a cost of about $125 a year.

Photographing or video taping each room in the house from every conceivable angle is the best way to insure that adequate compensation will be received in case of a tragedy. Place these pictures in a safety deposit box, noting date and original cost of each item. This may be the only way to recall and prove what was lost in a fire or burglary.

## CAR INSURANCE

Sticker shock occurs not only when a car is purchased, but also when car insurance is sought. In the past five years, rates have increased 55%, far more rapidly than the rate of inflation. Comparison shop, compare apples with apples. A wide variety of costs and benefits are available.

Two basic needs are met by car insurance:

### Liability Protection

We can never underestimate the value of such coverage. If we are driving and injure someone and are declared liable, costs can be staggering. In addition, such payments can continue for an extended period of time, long beyond the limits of the policy.

Liability insurance is mandatory in more than half of the states, but basic requirements are very modest, Typically, we are required to have liability of $25,000 per person, and $50,000 per accident for bodily injury and $10,000 for property damage. Not surprisingly, such coverage is called the 25-50-10 rule. Much risk accompanies such limits.

Authorities recommend instead a 100-300-50 policy. That is, $100,000 per person, $300,000 per accident and $50,000 for property damage. Raising the limits of a policy is not that expensive. As mentioned earlier, one creative solution is an umbrella coverage for both home and car, with liability limits of $1 million.

### Collision and Comprehensive Protection

Collision insurance pays for our car if an accident is our fault, or if it is caused by an at–fault driver who does not have insurance. The older the vehicle we are driving, the less important this kind of insurance becomes.

Comprehensive insurance protects us against the possibility of fire, theft, vandalism, etc. Again, the age of the car will be one major determining factor in the kind of coverage we carry.

## Some Ways to Save Money on Car Insurance

—Do not drive a car.

—Kind of car owned:

Buy cars which score well for safety and durability. Insurance companies have cut the rates for well over 100 models of cars, and added surcharges for almost a like number. For more information, contact:

Insurance Institution for Highway Safety
Attn: Publications Dept.
Watergate 600, Suite 300
Washington, D.C. 20037
(Ask for HLDI Composite Chart)

—Increased deductibles. The key to saving on car insurance premiums is the amount of the deductible and the amount of the damage we are willing to assume before insurance payments kick in. For instance, going from a $100 deductible to a $500 can slice an average of 30% off comprehensive and 25% off collision.

—Driving less: 7,500 or fewer miles driven in a year will sometimes qualify for lower premiums.

—Completing driving instruction: At least 21 states require a premium break for those who take a defensive driving course.

—Passive restraints: Items such as air bags or automatic safety belts may qualify for a deduction.

—Consolidating coverage: Insuring more than one vehicle with the same company or insuring more than just autos can save money.

—Abstinence: Non-smokers or non-drinkers can pay less.

—Longevity: Some companies give rate reductions for those 55 or older.

—Car-pooling: Some commuters who regularly rotate driving are eligible for reductions.

—Occupation: Some breaks are given to members of certain professions, those which have proven to be less accident prone.

—Good driving: Requirements vary but no moving violations or chargeable accidents for 36 months might qualify for lower premiums.

—Safeguarding a vehicle: Keeping a vehicle in a garage or in off-street parking or installing anti-theft devices may be rewarded.

—Special student rates: Drivers under the age of 25 have by far the highest rates. Discounts can help offset some of this cost for students who maintain a B average, make the honor roll, or who rank in the upper fifth of the class. In addition, parents' rates can be discounted if a child on their policy attends school 100 miles away or more, thus reducing the miles this child will drive.

—Yearly comparison shopping: Several phone calls each year to various car insurance companies at the time premium payments are due will find the lowest rates. By checking on a regular basis, substantial cost savings can be achieved.

## HEALTH INSURANCE

Coverage for medical care has changed drastically in recent years. Because of staggering costs, ground rules have been rearranged. We need to be well versed in the new playing field which has been established, so that we can plug any gaps which might exist in our own coverage. A major illness can be catastrophic if coverage is not adequate.

Two different approaches are most common:

### Fee for Service

This is a time tested traditional method of health care, where we are able to choose both our doctor and our hospital depending, of course, on where the doctor practices. Such coverage is normally provided by such huge companies as Blue Cross-Blue Shield or Aetna.

A deductible is included, often $150 to $250 per individual, $500 to $1,000 for a family. In addition, we are required to pay 20% to 25% of our own medical bills, up to a maximum of out-of-pocket costs, normally $3,000 to $4,000 a year. About half of all employers still pay the entire amount of health coverage, and a third provide coverage for all dependents.

However, more companies are now insisting that employees pay a part of the premium, generally from 5% to 20%. Dollar amounts can run as high as

$800 to $1,000 a year for a family of four, coming directly out of the paycheck. In recent years, these insurers will also not automatically pay full coverage for many charges. Partial payment is much more common.

Fee for service plans offer various options. For instance, a larger deduction can mean a lower premium, conversely a smaller deduction means a higher premium. Most experts recommend that a family be protected against high out of pocket costs, rather than trying to keep the premium low.

Basic to the fee for service plan is the opportunity to choose the doctor. In addition, a rare disease may mean combing the entire country for the right specialist, and the plan will provide coverage.

## Health Maintenance Organization (HMO)
## Preferred Provider Organization (PPO)

Under the above plans, all health care is generally covered, usually with no deductible and few co-payments. All preventative and routine care is included. Premiums are a bit less or about the same as the traditional fee for service. Most people join an HMO or PPO through an employer, and experience less out–of–pocket costs for medical care.

Chief among the disadvantages is the inability to have a completely free choice in a doctor and that specialists are often assigned if they are needed. However, many HMO's and PPO's will recommend outside specialists if they cannot handle the problem.

In addition, a disadvantage has been that the quality of the health care has varied widely. This can also happen in the fee for service option, but the individual has many more choices in that system.

On the other hand, a major advantage of an HMO or PPO is that a claim form very rarely needs to be completed. With the fee for service plan, medical bills must be saved, claim forms require the deciphering of often confusing rules that come from the insurance office.

## Cafeteria Plan

The fastest growing trend today is what is called a cafeteria plan, where employees can choose among a variety of options. Most of these are established in one of three ways.

—A choice is given of health, dental, life, retirement and disability coverage, as well as child care and other options, each with a different level of cost. The company will pick up the entire premium for the cheapest coverage, but not for any broader option.

—Credits are given the employee in order to buy the benefits desired. The employee may choose from a wide variety of choices and prices. All coverage which is more than the credited amount will be paid for by paycheck deductions.

—A basic benefit plan is given the employee at no cost, but many options are offered above and beyond the core plan.

Final Comments

When purchasing health insurance, group insurance is the most cost effective. Avoid mail order policies, or those offered through large organizations advertised in magazines or through direct mail. Many of these offers appeal to people who cannot get insurance elsewhere, so the high risk clientele means very high premiums.

For those who are above the age of 50 years, and cannot buy health insurance at a reasonable rate, contact the American Association of Retired People at 1–800–523–5800.

# INVESTING OUR SAVINGS

Once we have made the decision to save 10% of our income, we are suddenly faced with some new decisions. For instance, to just leave that money in a checking account is certainly not the best way to secure financial growth. Neither is it best to leave it in a cookie jar or under the mattress. The surest way to plan for the future is to utilize that money saved in the most productive way.

Investments can be incredibly complex. Many people spend a lifetime trying to master the nature and scope of the multitude of investments available. In this booklet, we will try to cut through the maze of possibilities and center on just a few of the basics. Most people can invest wisely by just pursuing the fundamentals. The playing field is wide enough for the more adventuresome to find plenty of room to roam, but most of us are much better off if we keep it very simple.

Investing for Income:

*Savings Account* – A traditional way to save. With money in the bank, we can continue to add by using our passbook, and we know the money is very safe. A modest rate of interest is paid, and we can just watch this amount grow whenever we have our passbook updated.

This kind of saving is often beneficial for children, helping them learn how to save so that interest can be earned. However, for most of the rest of us, savings accounts are not as good a place for maximizing earnings as they once were, many other sources give a much better return. Income on savings accounts is taxable.

*Checking Account* – Keeping money in a checking account used to be the worst possible investment, for no earning was possible. Now some checking accounts pay interest, which is a substantial improvement from the past. Interest rates are still in the very modest range, so it is better not to leave much money in these accounts. Also, earnings are taxable.

*Certificate of Deposit (CD)* – Similar to a savings account, except that the money and the interest rate are locked in for a specific period of time. The longer the term, the higher the interest. Withdrawing the money early will invoke a substantial penalty. CD's normally pay several percentage points above the inflation rate, and the earnings are taxed.

*Money Market Account* – A savings account where instant access is available to the money. Again, interest rates are usually higher than the traditional savings account or the checking accounts, but lower than CD's. Checks can be written against the money market account, but usually limited to larger amounts, $250 or $500.

*Treasury Bonds* - Because of increased risk, the interest rate on Treasury Bonds is slightly higher than CD's. Individual bonds come in minimum denominations of $1000. If purchased from a broker, you may have to pay a fee. Treasury Bonds have a fixed maturity of ten years to thirty years. Treasury Notes and Treasury Bills are available with shorter maturities. The interest rate is generally lower as the term of the obligation decreases. If a Treasury Bond, Bill or Note is sold prior to maturity, you may receive more or less than you initially paid for it, depending on current interest rates. When a Treasury Bond, Bill or Note matures, you will always receive the face amount of the obligation.

*Bond Funds* - In many cases, the best way to invest in bonds is through a bond fund, managed by a professional. A bond fund invests in many different individual bonds, and to some extent cushions the buyer from market fluctuations and interest rate changes. Bond funds often concentrate in a specific type of bond, such as U.S. Government bonds, high quality corporate bonds, or "junk" bonds.

*Municipal Bonds (Tax Free)* – Excellent investment for those in the higher tax brackets. Yields at one time were only about one-half of regular bonds, today the spread has narrowed considerably. Strangely enough, some municipal bonds even pay higher interest than the taxable T-bills.

*Annuity* - In some ways, this is the opposite of insurance. Insurance protects against an absence of income for survivors of those who live less years then expected. Annuities protect those who live longer than expected, by paying a regular amount for life from that which has been saved and compounded. The greatest advantage is that benefits are tax-deferred; no taxes are paid until the money is withdrawn, which can begin without penalty at age 59 1/2. A portion of the payments are also tax-free. There are many different types of annuities and many different ways to withdraw money from them, depending upon your needs.

Investing for Growth:

Sometimes it is possible to gain a financial windfall buying individual stocks. Going broke is also a distinct possibility. With the stock market crasn in October of 1987, we are more fully aware of how risky individual stocks can be. What goes up may also go down, and over a very short period of time. Knowing one's broker and his or her track record is also most important.

*Mutual Funds, Stock or Growth Funds* – For the average person, this is the best place to be in the stock market. Diversification is the basic strategy, shares are owned in a wide variety of companies. During the past generation, two major benefits of mutual funds have gained much attention — first, extremely impressive growth, and secondly, greatly reduced risk. Professional management makes the investing decision, all we have to do is send in a check.

Mutual funds are both "no-load" and "load". The no-load funds do not charge an initial sales fee, whereas load funds have such a fee. However, in some cases the no–load funds can actually be comparable to those of load, as additional charges are added. Also be aware that most funds charge an administrative fee of about 1% a year.

An effective strategy recommended by many professionals is to invest in the funds in a systematic, regular way. For instance, if we buy monthly or quarterly, we will buy some shares higher and some lower, depending on the going price. When we do it this way we end up with a lower average cost per share.

*Real Estate* – As discussed in an earlier chapter, the purchase of a home is probably the best overall investment that can be made. A second home or vacation place can also be a very solid investment, both in terms of the growth of assets and a provision for reduction of taxes. However, there is also the real possibility that by investing so strongly in real estate that we have little or nothing left to give or to realize other discretionary priorities.

In the final analysis, some combination of income and growth will be appropriate. Exact ratios will depend on what our short and long range goals might be, as well as age, health, and ability to endure risk. If risk makes us uncomfortable, then we will keep more of our investments in *income*; if we can endure more risk, then we will invest more strongly in *growth*.

# A MOST TAXING SITUATION

One day some of Jesus' enemies wanted to create a crisis for him. So they asked him the question, "Tell us, then, what is your opinion? Is it right to pay taxes to Caesar or not?" Talk about a no-win situation. If Jesus said that it was proper to pay taxes, especially the oppressive taxes his people were paying to hated Romans, he would be in deep trouble among all of the Jews.

On the other hand, if he said that it was not right to pay those taxes, he would be attacking the Roman ruler and thus be guilty of treason. A rather tight spot.

So Jesus gave the brilliant answer which has been passed down through the ages. "Give to Caesar that which is Caesar's and to God that which is God's." The people were amazed at this answer, and so are we. We never seem to be quite sure, however, how much should go to Caesar and how much to God.

Today it seems as if most of what we earn goes to Caesar. The government has discovered all sorts of ingenious ways to separate us from our money. We realize that we have some obligations because of living in this magnificent land, but when we see the many places our tax money is spent, or misspent, we tend to be less than thrilled by high tax rates.

The most recent tax bill of 1986 had two major effects. One, it lowered the tax rates for just about everyone. On the other hand, because of the elimination of many deductions, many people are paying more taxes. Fairness is often in the eye of the beholder, so it is entirely possible that we will never have a tax system which everyone thinks is fair.

As Christians we are called to be citizens both of heaven and also of this earth. This means that we are to fulfill the various responsibilities of citizenship. At times certain parts of the Christian community have chosen to bow out of the political process and have become isolated from the world, because of some beliefs that the process is evil, tainted or irrelevant. But by and large, Christians see the need to be responsible citizens and to pay a fair share of taxes.

At the same time, we need to affirm again that we are not called to pay more than we owe. There is nothing especially Christian or even very smart about paying more taxes than we are assessed. In fact, if we are Christian stewards we are very aware that there are many places this money could be used more efficiently and wisely than by overpaying the government. We pay our rightful share, but no more.

In order to make sure we do not overpay, we need to take the necessary planning steps. At the beginning of each year, we need to lay out the various parts of our financial plan, projected income and expenses, as well as the tax obligations we will be facing. Keeping taxes at a minimum will be a part of that process.

Basically, only two ways remain for us to reduce taxes. The first is to reduce income, perhaps not an acceptable strategy for most of us. However, there are ways to reduce taxable income which do make sense and are explained in other chapters in this booklet.

The other way to reduce taxes is through the spending of money, as in tax sheltered investments. However, much of this effort is very risky, and much money has been lost in speculative ventures. The tax law of 1986 did us a favor; by eliminating many of the tax sheltered options it saved many of us who are not especially sophisticated in financial matters considerable risk and loss. It's not often we thank Uncle Sam for eliminating deductions, but this may be one of these times.

Huge volumes can be written on tax law. This booklet wants simply to affirm that reducing our tax load will give us more discretionary income to give away or to spend. Wise planning is the key to tax reduction.

For information on the present tax rates, consult the Internal Revenue Service.

# IS THERE LIFE AFTER WORK?

Imagine the following vision! Warm weather during the middle of the coldest winter...lush golf courses surrounded by the bluest of skies and ocean, perhaps a condo or motor home in the picture. Retirement is almost heavenly, health is good, finances are secure, mental faculties are excellent. Work is just a memory. Now there is time for so many opportunities to celebrate life.

Sound familiar? Many variations can surround that basic theme, but the ideal of a beautiful retirement is common to most of us. However, this kind of scenario will not happen by accident, an intentional strategy must be a priority during most of the working years. Some of the foundation for retirement is already in place, but putting together a very specific plan is much better than having no plan at all.

Americans have traditionally built their retirement income on three different planks. These include Social Security, a company pension and one's own investments. More details are as follows:

## Social Security

In order to ease our minds, the first statement that needs to be made is that the Social Security System is presently in excellent financial condition. Some of the horror stories which have been circulated in recent years are patently false, the system now has a huge surplus and is presently providing support for our huge federal budget. Social Security will have more than enough to meet all obligations in the immediate future.

Social Security expects people to retire at age 65. However, today almost 70% of the people who file for benefits do so earlier than age 65. More than 50% file at age 62.

Filing at age 62 has both negative and positive effects. Benefits are 20% lower at this earlier age. People born after 1937 will be faced with an even steeper bite in the future. Retirement age has been set by Congress to rise to age 67 between the years of 2003 and 2027. At that point the penalty for retiring at age 62 will be 30%.

On the other hand, retiring at age 62 means collecting benefits three years earlier. The cumulative amount of these three additional years means that those who retire at age 65 will not catch up until age 77.

Checking records with the Social Security Administration every few years is good common sense. Mistakes have been known to occur, and it is better to discover the errors earlier rather than later, when better records should be available.

To verify an account, send in a card for that purpose entitled *Request for Statement of Earnings*, Form SSA-7004. Call, visit or write the local office for the form. Within four to six weeks after sending the card, a year by year listing of all earnings for the past several years will be sent, as well as a career lump sum. Check the figures against recent W-2 forms for accuracy.

## Pensions

Social Security benefits are not sufficient for most of us in retirement. Thus, we turn to the second of the planks, that of the company pension. Two kinds are dominant.

*Defined benefit plan* – This is funded entirely out of the company's pocket.

Most companies calculate pension benefits as a percentage of salary during the highest paid three to five years, multiplied by the number of years of service. These benefits are then reduced by a portion of the Social Security benefits.

A typical pension formula awards employees an amount roughly equal to 1% of monthly salary multiplied by the number of years of employment.

*Defined contribution plan* – In addition, most companies offer plans by which employees can set aside retirement money on a tax–deferred basis. Most common among these is the *401 (k) plan*, which directs that at least some of the money put in this fund will reduce salary reported to IRS. A large majority of companies also match contributions of the employee, chipping in 25 to 50 cents or more on the dollar.

Pensions are basically safe. Forty-one million workers who are covered by some kind of defined benefit plan have little to worry about. At the present time, huge surpluses exist in most pension plans. If underfunded, the company itself is required to contribute enough money to pay the pension.

If for some reason the company should go out of business, a last line of defense has been established.

*Pension Benefit Guarantee Corporation* – A federally charted insurance company which is responsible for making good on unfilled promises by private pensions, up to a maximum annual benefit of around $22,900. That is enough for all but the highest paid employees.

Early retirement is growing. Many companies are encouraging this trend by holding out rather attractive carrots, making retirement before age 65 much more appealing.

The best way to maximize a pension is to spend long years with the same company. Jumping from one employer to another will most likely bring a lower pension. Leaving a job before five years are completed may even mean leaving most of the pension behind, since an employee may not be fully vested. An employee should not leave a job until proper information is received about the pension benefits. This may prevent a costly mistake.

Pension money will not equal an employee's salary. Even after 25 or 30 years with the same company, a pension income will still not be more than 40 to 50% of pre–retirement salary.

Many experts suggest that between 70 and 80% of present income will be necessary when retirement comes. If this is accurate, pension money and Social Security will not be sufficient. Therefore, a third plank in this foundation is crucial, involving other savings and investments.

## Pension Savings And Investments

*The 401 (k) plan* was mentioned previously. Chief among its advantages is that it allows an employee to build retirement savings through a tax deferred device. From one to ten per cent of pre-tax salary, up to $7,313 in 1988, can be invested in an array of stocks, bonds and mutual funds. The company's contribution was not limited by the 1986 tax law.

Money contributed to such a plan goes into a professionally managed retirement fund, and no income tax will be paid on contributions of earnings until the money is withdrawn. Before the age of 59 1/2, the employee can withdraw only his or her contributions, and income tax plus a 10% penalty will be paid. However, that penalty will be waived if the money is used to pay medical expenses which exceed 7.5% of adjusted gross income.

*Keogh Plan* – Here is a tax-deferred plan for those who are self-employed. Up to $30,000 or 13.04% of net self-employment income, whichever is less, can be placed in a profit sharing Keogh plan, and a second Keogh up to a total of 20% can be set aside. A defined benefit plan may allow even more. Again, no income tax is paid on contributions or earnings until the money is withdrawn.

*Individual Retirement Account (IRA)* – Many people believe that the most recent tax law did away with the IRA. For some people it did. But IRA tax deductions are still fully available for most people. For those who are not presently covered by a company pension or Keogh plan, both husband and wife can each still deduct a full $2,000 contribution, just as before. No income ceiling has been established.

If either spouse has a company pension, IRA deductions depend entirely on income. A single person who has an adjusted gross income below $25,000 can still take a full $2,000 IRA. For every five dollars of adjusted gross income over $25,000, one dollar is lost of IRA deduction. $35,000 is the limit for a single person for any IRA deductions.

Married persons who have a combined adjusted gross income totaling less than $40,000 can still deduct two $2,000 amounts. For every five dollars of adjusted gross income over $40,000, both lose one dollar of IRA deductibility. When the adjusted gross income reaches $50,000, there is no longer any deduction.

For those who are no longer eligible for a tax deferred IRA deduction, money can still be contributed to an IRA, where the earnings will continue to accumulate tax free until the money is withdrawn.

Withdrawing the Money

New guidelines have been established by the IRS. While withdrawals may begin at the age of 59 1/2, mandatory withdrawals must begin to take place by the age of 70 1/2. Under–withdrawals after that age will result in a tax equal to 50% of the shortfall.

The amount of the minimum that can be withdrawn is based on a rather complicated formula that depends on age as well as the age of the designated beneficiary. For most specific information the best place to look is the IRS Publication No. 575, *Pension and Annuity Income*.

How the invested money is received is most important. Withdrawing more money than is necessary will mean paying needless taxes, perhaps even raising one's tax bracket. Investments should not be drawn down more quickly than needed, which will require a rather careful financial plan.

At present, if adjusted gross income including tax exempt income and half of the Social Security exceed $32,000 for married couples filing jointly, and $25,000 for a single, up to one half of the Social Security benefits are taxable.

## Continued Medical Care

Age 65 qualifies one for medicare. A growing number of companies will continue coverage for retirees over the age of 60 to plug into medicare benefits. Employees with such coverage most likely do not need to purchase a separate medigap policy.

A variety of insurance policies are available to the retired populace. Younger persons tend to pay less than those who are older. For more specific information, contact the American Association of Retired Persons.

Retirement can be one of the most enjoyable periods of life, or it can also be one of the most miserable. Plan ahead, develop a strategy to create very positive and creative years once the pressure of everyday work is over. God has prepared for the time after retirement, but each of us must prepare for those years just prior to our life with our Creator.

# RISKS OF RETIREMENT

For those who have sufficient funds in the three planks described in the previous chapter, retirement can be an exciting and rewarding time. But there is always a dark cloud on the horizon, namely, the possibility of serious illness. Each of us will die of something, and some of us will face long and costly struggles with illness.

Nursing homes provide both the possibility of excellent care for those with debilitating illnesses, but also the potential for the greatest cost. At the present time, some 2.3 million Americans are living in nursing homes. The number could double in the next 30 years. Average costs in 1988 are $22,000 a year. With moderate inflation, by the year 2018 the cost could be $55,000.

Where do we turn for help? What kind of preparation can we make now for the potential of huge costs later on? The subject is very complex.

## What is Now Covered?

*Medicare* is designed for those who are age 65 or above, and for the most part covers major hospital expenses. Costs up to 60 days are covered, with an initial deductible of $540, with an additional 30 days in which the patient pays $135 a day. After being out of the hospital for 60 days, a patient may return with the above benefits being back in force.

Medicare pays skilled nursing care only in approved facilities, with 100% of eligible expenses covered for the first 20 days, and all but $67.50 a day for the next 80 days. No custodial or intermediate care is covered. Nothing is covered after the 100 days are up. Some home care is provided, but with many limitations.

A *Supplementary Medical Insurance* is also available through Social Security. Premiums and benefit information can be secured through the Social Security Administration.

*Medicaid.* Most people are not poor when they enter a nursing home, but they become poor soon after, due to the cost of health services. Medicaid is a combined federal and state program which finances health services for the poor, and pays approximately one half of the 38 billion dollar price tag for nursing home costs.

Once a person's assets drop below a predetermined amount, normally $1,800 in individual assets, not counting one's house, car and home furnishings, Medicaid covers skilled, intermediate and custodial care. Part-time nursing and home health aid if requested by a physician are also covered.

The most recent catastrophic bill included a *Spousal Impoverishment Clause*. This means that a husband and wife can divide their assets in half. The half that is controlled by the person in the nursing home will be drawn down until Medicaid takes over. The other spouse can keep the other half, with some specific minimums and maximums, but will be required to pay something toward the nursing home care. Some states are attempting to remove this requirement.

Generally, three types of nursing home care is provided. Each of these has different coverages, so it is important that we understand the nature of each.

*Skilled Nursing Care*. Care must be prescribed by a doctor, given by a skilled nurse, and be available 24 hours a day. Such a facility must be licensed by the state and daily medical records kept on each person.

*Intermediate Nursing Care*. Care of a nurse may be required, but the level of care is less than skilled. The nurse may be on hand only to give injections or change bandages. Such a facility may be licensed and may provide post hospital and rehabilitative nursing care.

*Custodial Nursing Care*. A patient is helped with routine activities, such as getting out of bed, walking, bathing, or eating. This care may be given by people without professional skills or training.

States vary in the types of care. Minnesota, for instance, has essentially eleven levels of care and eleven different rates, all dictated by the care needs of the individual. State and local laws should be researched in order to have a clear understanding of the care which is available.

In recent years, *private long term insurance policies* for the elderly have grown tremendously. Some 70 different companies offer them. However, among these policies is a wide range of benefits and restrictions. The buyer must be very careful to understand everything about the policy and be assured that it will do what the buyer wants it to do.

Obviously, the younger a person purchases a policy, the lower the premium. Most experts recommend that this not be purchased until age 55 or 60, unless there is a way to keep the benefits current with inflation. However, people who have very modest assets should probably not buy these policies. They will quickly qualify for Medicaid benefits should they need to spend time in a nursing home.

What are some benefits that should be included?
—A daily nursing home benefit of at least $80
—A waiting period of no more than 20 days
—Unlimited benefits for as long as needed
—Full benefits for skilled, intermediate, and custodial care
—Home care benefits, without requiring nursing home stay or hospital stay
—Guaranteed renewability of the policy
—Coverage for Alzheimers disease

Life Care Communities

A new phenomenon has appeared on the horizon in recent years, life care communities. An estimated 90,000 people now live in these facilities. In exchange for a one time payment of anywhere from $16,000 to $175,000 (average $35,000), people purchase a contract which guarantees them food, housing and if necessary, nursing home care for the rest of their life. The idea is most appealing. By selling a home and using part or all of the money to buy a contract, protection is guaranteed.

But is it? Many of these communities have been found to be on extremely shaky financial ground, and a number of them have defaulted. Again, regulations of such offerings vary from state to state. People considering such a possibility should do much investigating before taking such a step. Look at the financial resources, check all of the regulatory agencies, do comparison shopping. This is too important a decision to rush headlong into the wrong place.

In essence, the coverage for old-age illnesses is a highly complex issue. Some of the places to contact for more information include:

Social Security Administration

State Department of Health

Consumers Report Magazine, April, 1988

Local Senior Citizen Organizations

American Association of Retired Persons
(Health Advocacy Services)
1909 K Street N.W.
Washington, D.C. 20049

ABA Commission on the Legal Problems of Elderly
American Bar Association
1800 M Street N.W.
Washington, D.C. 20036

# WE CANNOT TAKE IT WITH US

The old cartoon says it best. As the hearse rolled by carrying the casket of the wealthiest man in town, one onlooker said to another, "How much did he leave?" The reply, "He left it all." Someday we will leave it all. The only question that remains is where we will leave it.

Some people because of laziness or sloppy planning leave much of their estate to those who are not even listed in the will. As one money manager said only somewhat facetiously, "Estate planning is the orderly and systematic disposition of one's property into fees and commissions."

Others will leave most of their assets to the government, in the form of estate and other taxes. Very few among us would choose that as the proper place for our estate.

As mentioned in a previous chapter, Christians have often wondered about the legitimacy of avoiding taxes, of taking advantage of the various charitable giving deductions. Isn't this a bit unethical?

But what we need to understand is that the tax structure of our country has been designed in order to accomplish some very specific goals. Some of those goals are financial, others are social and humanitarian. As a part of the tax code, certain policies have been established deliberately to encourage generous charitable giving.

Somewhere along the line, the government decided that nonprofit organizations could accomplish certain tasks much more efficiently and humanely than could the government. So the tax code was established to encourage us to give to charity, both while we are alive and also through our estate. Christians should be most grateful for this open door. Certainly many nations in the world have far different priorities.

Therefore, when we plan our estate, we should look at ways to give to others while at the same time using the particular incentives given by Uncle Sam. The chapter on Charitable Giving gives more details as to the implementation of such planning.

When we consider all of the various pieces of estate planning, three particular needs come to the fore:

—We consider our own financial needs for the rest of our life. We will want, as much as possible, to provide an adequate income for ourselves for our remaining working years, as well as after we retire. Investing our assets as wisely as possible, we are ready for what is to come. Part of this planning looks for ways to decrease our current and future taxes, so that we will have as much discretionary income for ourselves and others.

— We consider the needs of our family. We want to leave our loved ones sufficient financial resources which provide for them and protect them after our own death. A whole range of creative options are available for consideration in carrying out this goal.

— We consider the needs of others, of the many worthwhile charitable organizations in our midst. Christians will especially wish to demonstrate the same priorities of giving and sharing in death as they have evidenced in life.

## Creating a Will

Basic to all estate planning is the creation of a will. Anyone who does not have a will in this day and age is playing a dangerous game of roulette with the future. Our commitment to Christian stewardship seems to demand that we have a will, so that we can make sure that God, our family and others will receive as much as possible.

What makes this so urgent is that an estimated 70% of those who died in a recent year did not have a will. Imagine, 70%! In addition, of the 30% who have wills, many of them are not pleased with the specific provisions of that will. In fact, they would like to change it. Still others have not updated their will recently, especially after the many crucial tax changes of recent years.

For those who do not have a will, they should be reminded that the state in which they reside has very thoughtfully prepared a will for them. What is in the will may be a secret. We will never be asked to sign it, but it is in effect nevertheless. Government has set into place the mechanism to decide who gets everything we have if we have not done this on our own.

A will is a last will and testament. Another way of stating this is to say that it is our final *testimony*. A testimony is a statement of faith. Our will is stating publicly what we believe, our basic values and priorities. What an opportunity to share something about the Lordship of Christ, and to make sure that our will is a response to our basic Christian faith.

Many of the decisions in our will revolve around how much of our assets we will leave to our children. Most of the time the majority of the assets go directly to the surviving spouse, but when the second spouse dies, then the major transfer takes place. Where do we want our assets to go?

*What is a Will?* The Lutheran Church has a very helpful brochure about wills, making the following points.

— A will demonstrates living and caring, providing a message from us to those who will survive us.

— A will brings order and direction to the estate. Making a will prompts us to evaluate our possessions.

— A will may preserve the value of our possessions. It provides for the prompt and inexpensive transfer of our assets to others. Without a will, the state will usually distribute this property. Court costs and taxes are usually significantly higher in the absence of a will.

— A will protects those whom we love. Replacement parents can be named for minor children, as well as providing them with basic financial care. Plans are also set up so that children will receive the finances when they are best able to handle them.

— A will personalizes the transfer of possessions. Only through a will can we give personal items to others.

— A will prevents many family conflicts, providing a very clear direction for those who survive.

— A will may provide a specific financial plan for our loved ones. In other words, regular income can be designated for our spouse or other heirs.

For those who do not have a will, the time to act on this is now. If we do not already have an attorney, we can ask friends for recommendations. The cost for a rather uncomplicated will should be in the neighborhood of $100 to $500. If the financial picture is rather complex, the cost could be higher. However, a will is very cost effective when compared with the costs involved without one.

Basic Information For the Will

For an attorney to be able to draw up a will, some basic information will be needed. Before making a contact, pull together the following data to help in the creation of the will.

— Social Security numbers

— Date and place of birth

— Information on marriage and any previous marriage

— Income tax information

— Health status

— Information about children, including educational goals

— Information on both sets of grandparents, both sets of brothers and sisters

— Any money which may be inherited

— Armed forces records, serial number and dates of service

— List of all bank accounts, savings certificates, treasury bonds, money market accounts, stocks and bonds, including purchase price, date purchased, present market value, and how asset is titled

— Mortgages owned, market value information and how asset is titled

— Complete information on other property owned and how the asset is titled

— Information and policy number of all insurance policies

— Balance sheets and profit-loss statement of any business owned

— Information if you have ever lived in a community property state

— Copies of pension plans, benefits and stock options

— Title information of automobiles

— List of other major possessions: boats, trailers, china, art, family heirlooms, collections, copyrights, patents

— List of debts

— Any safe deposit vaults and location of other important documents

—Accounting of any substantial gifts made in the past

—Names and addresses for first and second choices for guardian of minor children or for executor

—Any special arrangements for funerals, burial or organ donation

—Any special provision that would result in the children being treated other than equally

A will is an essential part of a financial plan. The time to create that will or to update an existing will is now. There is no time to lose.

# WHAT TO DO WHEN OUR SHIP COMES IN

America continues to be the land of opportunity. Certainly this is not true for everyone. One of the tragedies of our society is the number of people who have been left out. Yet for many the doors are wide open for finding financial rewards far beyond our fondest dreams. Some people seem to have the gift of earning money. Why this is the case, we are not quite sure. But some most assuredly have a golden touch.

The Biblical writers struggle with the impact of wealth, and the personal cost necessary to find it. One of the most striking passages is in I Timothy 6:10.

"People who want to get rich fall into temptation and a trap and into many foolish and harmful desires that plunge men into ruin and destruction. For the love of money is a root of all kinds of evil. Some people, eager for money, have wandered from the faith and pierced themselves with many griefs."

Powerful words! Money itself is not seen as evil, but the quest for riches is seen as the danger. In other words, the path toward wealth is lined with much potential for abuse.

At the same time, this same chapter speaks a strong word to those who are already wealthy, I Timothy 6:17.

"Command those who are rich in this present world not to be arrogant, nor to put their hope in wealth, which is so uncertain, but to put their hope in God, who richly provides us with everything for our enjoyment. Command them to do good, to be rich in good deeds, and to be generous and willing to share. In this way they will lay up treasure for themselves as a firm foundation for the coming age, so that they may take hold of the life which is truly life."

When we think of a lifestyle for the rich and famous, the words just quoted are most appropriate. Of course, they are quite at odds with so much of what we see paraded in the media. What should a Christian do with an abundance of wealth? Some suggestions:

## Realize That Everything is a Gift

God is the owner. We have been given some assets to manage for just a short period of time. A steward recognizes that everything has come from God, a wonderful gift. The ultimate measure of a life is not how much one accumulates, but how much one gives. We live each day with thanksgiving, humility and praise, finding ways to use the wealth to the glory of God.

## Make Giving Count

Give generously on a regular basis to the local congregation. Step forward when any special needs arise, be a leader. Watch the world and the church be a better place because of our generosity.

A recent newspaper article highlighted a form of giving called the MacArthur Fellowship. Each year 25 or so experts in one field or another are given fellowships which range from $30,000 to $75,000 a year for five years. No strings are attached, no accounting is asked for. Gifted people who have had to struggle for funds are given financial help to encourage them to maximize their own talents and visions. A similar program in the Christian arena could provide a dramatic impact throughout the entire church.

Creative giving opportunities are all about us. People who have accumulated much can make a dramatic difference.

## Find A Financial Adviser Who Understands Charitable Giving

Unfortunately, many millions of dollars are not given to worthwhile charities each year because financial advisers simply do not understand (and sometimes do not care) about understanding this complex field. A Christian with wealth should seek the best financial help possible, especially when it comes to giving money or property away. If finding someone is difficult, contact the national offices of the Lutheran church for advice.

## For Business Owners, Consider the Five Per Cent Plan

A growing number of major companies are setting aside a portion of their earnings to give away. Five per cent seems to be the percentage many of them have decided to give of pre-tax income. This money funds a wide range of community projects, giving back to that same community which has provided a place and an arena for the business to flourish.

This will take enlightened leadership at the top of the business, those who see giving to others as a priority. Christian businesspersons can give not only out of personal wealth, but also out of company earnings. Needless to say, the potential of such gifts for many corporations is astounding.

## Become An Evangelist for Giving

Very often those who have wealth associate with others in the same circumstances. A Christian with wealth who understands giving can have a potent influence on others with money. Leading by example and by personal contact can inspire others to give most generously. Wealth can talk to wealth.

## Give More Than 10% a Year

We begin at 10%, but we don't necessarily end there. For those of us who have seen our ship come in, giving should go way beyond the norm. An increase of 1% or 2% a year would be a realistic goal.

We read much these days about those in our society who have accumulated the most. Fortunes of one billion, 800 million, 600 million, etc. are not all that unusual. Some magazines keep score of such things, almost like batting averages, and compute them on an annual basis.

How much is too much? How much is enough? Lewis Lapham in an incisive book entitled *Money and Class in America* makes the following comments. Nobody ever has enough. It is characteristic of the rich person or nation to think that they do not have enough of anything. No matter what their income, a depressing amount of Americans believe that if only they had twice as much they would inherit the estate of happiness promised them by the Declaration of Independence.

The doubling principle holds as firm as the price of emeralds. A person who receives $15,000 a year is sure that sorrow can be relieved with $30,000 a year, someone with $1 million a year knows that all would be well if the income was $2 million a year. It is precisely this belief that causes so much envy and rage, and why most of us remain dissatisfied.

Why not begin to give this money away? No one can bring it along when this life is over. We do not have to be dead to give generously. The time to give it away is now, when we can see how much good that giving can do.

## Retiring Early? Do Not Spend Every Moment Playing

For those of us who are wealthy enough to retire at an early age, the temptation is to spend the rest of our days playing. Certainly some time to relax and enjoy the new time and prosperity is deserved. But we continue to be stewards of our time as well as of our money.

Most likely the person with wealth has been given many talents and abilities. These can still be used for a wide variety of purposes. Giving oneself to the church as well as to other non–profit organizations can be as rewarding as giving money.

## Don't Leave Everything to Children and Grandchildren

One of the worst things that can happen to young people is for them to become instantly wealthy. Our world is littered with people who have been given huge inheritances and they have wasted their lives away. It is better to give them limited funds, help in college costs, perhaps a vacation home or some investments or a trust.

Anyone who is considering leaving substantial wealth to heirs should ask the question, "What kind of a person would I have been if I had inherited wealth? Would I have accomplished even a fraction of what I have been able to do?" Most likely the answer is no. The best thing for children or grandchildren is to earn their own way, not to receive money that is not earned.

## Be Aware of the Estate Tax

For those who have assets totaling more than $1.2 million, the estate tax can be as high as 55%. In other words, someone with substantial wealth will give more than half of it away once the $1.2 million dollar figure is surpassed. Needless to say, most people can find better places for that money than watching it be eaten up in taxes.

Consider giving everything over the $1.2 million away. That is more than enough to take care of the heirs, so why not give the rest of it away?

An example is a woman by the name of Emma Howe. She was born in 1890 near Barron, Wisconsin, the sixth of 13 children. She was raised in a very strait–laced, pure blooded German Lutheran family and knew poverty first hand.

At the age of 13 she left school to go to work, and shortly thereafter came to St. Paul to find a job. Her first job was with the newly formed company called Deluxe Check Printers. Right from the beginning, Emma began purchasing stock in the company, and often when the business was short of cash, she was paid in stock.

Since those beginning years, the stock has split ten for one three times, and two for one four times. When Emma died, she owned 709,000 shares of Deluxe Check stock, worth almost 40 million dollars. She gave most of the money away to a foundation which will use the money to serve the needs of the poor and the disadvantaged. Imagine, well over 30 million given away to others, rather than leaving all that wealth to heirs. A beautiful example!

## Give Pace Setting Gifts

Whenever there is a major fund drive, a building program at a local congregation, the construction of a YMCA, or numerous other endeavors, a rule of thumb is that a 10% gift is needed up front. If one million dollars is needed, then a gift of $100,000 will make it much more possible to reach the goal.

People of wealth should consider giving that lead gift whenever possible. Not only is the giving of the gift a strong response to the Christian gospel, but it also has a way of freeing up many more gifts as well. Once other people see such a generous response, this encourages and enables many others to follow suit.

A Lutheran congregation was in the middle of a 5 million dollar building program. Efforts were not bearing much fruit at first, only about $500,000 had been pledged at the outset. Suddenly a million dollar gift was pledged, two one-half million dollar gifts, and one for a quarter million. 2 1/2 million dollars was given by four families. The fund drive literally took off from there, and went well over the 5 million goal.

Up-front large gifts are crucial for any kind of fund drive. Those who have been given wealth should consider being counted right from the beginning, knowing that this will motivate many others to give generously.

Wealth can bring about arrogance, a sense of power, and greed. But it can also be used thankfully and gratefully to change this world in which we live. Giving brings more joy than almost anything in this world. Those with riches should have opportunity to experience every bit of joy possible.

# THE COSTS OF DIVORCE

The marriage vows are said with intensity and meaning, "For better, for worse; for richer, for poorer; in sickness and in health, until death parts us." Just about every couple truly believes every word that is said and has a vision of a lifetime of love and growth. God is at the center of the marriage, the future is very bright indeed.

However, for a variety of reasons, many of these marriages which begin with such promise eventually come apart. What has happened is actually a death, the death of a relationship, the death of a dream, the death of a marriage. One or both of the partners has been abused or abandoned. Not even the power of God or the resources of the Christian faith have been able to heal the split.

The cost of divorce is high. Each partner has experienced devastating pain and loss, often in isolation. The church has often been less than helpful. At the time of a physical death, the Christian community usually responds magnificently, reaching out in love at the visitation, funeral and well beyond. At the death of a marriage, people often back away rather than come to support. In some ways, divorce is more painful than losing a spouse by death.

The cost is also very high to the children of this marriage. Torn apart is that security net so important to every child, the security of a united home. Often they have been pulled in one direction or the other, or both at the same time, looked to for support by hurting parents who cannot give very much in return. Just about everyone loses in a divorce.

Financial costs of divorce are substantial. In more recent years, a definite shift has taken place in the nature of divorce settlements. At one time most debates centered around the issue of who was at fault, now the discussion has shifted to a negotiation over assets.

Divorce has increasingly been viewed by the courts as well as by the divorcing people themselves as the breakup of an economic partnership, similar to the dissolution of a business. We may see this as most unfortunate, but with the increasing affluence of many American families, this development may have been inevitable. Of course, with such high financial stakes present, the cost of divorce is rising.

Laws are changing in the area of divorce at a rapid pace. What is true one year may be completely changed the next. Therefore, it is of the utmost importance to find an attorney who has the knowledge and the understanding of this complex field. A high trust level is essential; if this can be attained, then the proceedings will be far easier and most likely less costly.

## Attorney Costs

Unless the divorce arrangements are relatively simple, no children, minimal assets, the cost of legal fees can become very expensive. Costs can range from $500 to $1,000 for the least complicated, up to $10,000 or even beyond for divorces where the assets are considerable or the hostility very high.

A retainer should be signed with an attorney listing all of the fees which have been negotiated. Insist on a regular billing of the costs incurred, so that information is up-to-date. Before any additional work is requested of the attorney, know the financial implications and how the money will be paid.

Finding the right attorney is most important. A new trend which is emerging is the move toward more specialists in the law arena. Family law specialists will eventually become much more prominent in this field, with specific training and certification required.

Interviews should be conducted with more than one possibility. Most of the time these initial meetings are without charge. A search should be made for someone who is well versed in divorce law, and who seems to truly be interested in a fair and equitable settlement.

The best place to find recommendations for such an attorney is through friends who have also gone through a similar experience, or from a friend you trust who has had good results from a specific person. An experienced and understanding attorney can often save money by settling a divorce in a quick and efficient manner. Make sure that all costs are completely understood and agreed to before an attorney is retained.

Resist the temptation to find an attorney with the personality of a pit bull. Sometimes the anger is so close to the surface in a divorcing partner that the major goal seems to be to severely punish the other person. Thus, an attorney is chosen who is particularly adept at attacking. Not only will this drive up costs, but it usually also means that everyone will lose.

Costs of a divorce can be minimized primarily by avoiding as much divisiveness as possible. The more the spouses can work out the solutions to the financial settlement by themselves, the lower the cost. If the attorneys must become involved in detailed negotiations, or if the issues can only be settled by a court fight, prepare to pay a high price.

Divorce Mediation

Mediation is relatively new to the divorce field. Here a neutral party, usually a mental health professional or an attorney specializing in family law, helps couples work out an agreement but has no power to make binding decisions. Mediation will not work if one or both spouses wish to drag out the process or is too bitter to cooperate.

Such mediation assistance can be much less expensive than working through attorneys; however, at the same time it can be more expensive. The mediator's fee, which can average between $50 and $150 an hour, is only one dimension. The agreement then needs to be taken to the respective attorneys of the divorcing spouses, and if there are problems with the proposal, then both attorneys will need to spend time. Thus, it is possible to pay three people instead of two. Each situation is different. At any rate, be sure to comparison shop before making a final decision.

For help in finding a mediator, consult the following:

Academy of Family Mediators
P.O. Box 10501
Eugene, OR 97440
503–345–1205

Procedures for Divorce

—Petition for Dissolution of a Marriage – This action starts the proceedings.

—Temporary Hearing, Application for Temporary Relief – Decisions are made to protect each of the spouses during the time of divorcing, particularly in the area of children and finances.

—Stipulation – Both parties come to an agreement on the settlement. The following areas are considered:

1. Child Support
2. Child Custody
3. Household Goods
4. The Homestead, place of residence
5. Medical and Dental Insurance for Minor Children
6. Automobiles
7. Checking and Savings Accounts
8. Debts
9. Profit Sharing Plan
10. Dependents for tax purposes
11. Life Insurance
12. Spousal Maintenance
13. Retirement Plan
14. Attorney's Fees
15. Non–Marital Property
16. Medical Insurance

—Court – A judgment is made concerning the stipulation.

## Specific Financial Decisions – Division of Assets

Most states have some kind of formula to help the spouses split the assets. Actual wording requires a fair, though not necessarily equal, division of property. What fair means, of course, is where the arguments begin.

In the past, homemakers have suffered a lack of fairness. Establishing that they contributed 50% of the financial assets has been difficult to prove. Lately, however, states are giving more weight to dividing property based on both monetary and non–monetary contributions. In other words, running a household or raising children has monetary value.

Most states exclude from the division of assets any property which belonged to one or the other spouse before the marriage, or any major bequests or gifts given specifically to one or the other during the marriage.

## Spousal Maintenance (Alimony)

State law in Texas prohibits alimony, but in the other 49 this becomes a crucial issue. Key factors in making determinations include the needs and financial abilities of each spouse, as well as age and health.

Courts in recent years have granted much less alimony. In the past, wives usually received payments until they remarried or died. Today this happens only in situations where divorces end very long marriages and where the wife has never worked outside the home, having rather poor prospects of being self supporting.

Couples married less than seven years, where the wife is relatively young and healthy, will most often have no alimony at all. Marriage of more than seven years will often require permanent spousal maintenance.

Rehabilitative alimony is the newest option, where alimony is paid until the non–working spouse can support himself or herself. Such alimony may be paid until that spouse can secure the necessary training or finds a job, or it may even become permanent. Laws are changing so quickly, it is most difficult to make any general rule.

Alimony is still tax deductible after the bill of 1986 for the one who pays, but it is taxed income for the one who receives. IRS restricts the amount that can be deducted for alimony during the first three years of the settlement.

## Child Support

Specifics vary from state to state. Historically, some of these payments could be treated as alimony, but no longer. Any payments that will eventually be reduced when a child reaches a certain age can never be alimony.

The income tax exemption for the child generally goes to the parent with whom the child lives, regardless of which parent provides most of the support. This exemption can be shifted to the other parent by agreement with a signed waiver from the custodial parent that is attached to the tax return. Tax reform has almost doubled the value of the exemption to $2,000 in 1989, so this decision takes on increased tax importance.

Both parents are expected to share in paying child support in accordance with means and ability. One of the tragedies of our time is how many fathers have abandoned this responsibility, forcing the ex-spouse as well as the children to pay a very high price. As a general rule, child support ends when a child reaches 18. If both parents are college graduates, a court may require the wealthier parent to underwrite the expense of higher education as a part of the divorce agreement.

We hear many reports today of the number of divorced parents who are not living up to the divorce agreement which was made, especially in the area of child support. Many states have become much more intentional in forcing compliance. For instance, in some states automatic withholding from paychecks is being tested. In addition, applicants for jobs in many areas of the country are being asked about outstanding child support obligations, so the employer is aware of the situation before hiring.

## Dividing the Residence

In a majority of situations, though not as often as in the past, if there are still children at home the largest asset, the residence, will be awarded to the wife with outright ownership. Or she may continue to live in the house, with the husband paying the mortgage until the children graduate from high school. At that time, the house may be sold and the proceeds split.

The most recent tax bill of 1986 makes property settlements more costly for the spouse who receives the assets. This spouse is responsible for all gain on the property, even that which happened before the transfer. Before the new tax law, 60% of the appreciation was tax free, now 100% is taxed.

Transfer of property also has new rules. In the past this was viewed as a sale. For instance, if a husband gave stock to his wife, he would have to pay taxes on the profits. Now, however, these are treated as gifts and neither party pays taxes at the time of divorce. Taxes will someday be paid, of course, so highly appreciated assets are worth less than might be expected, because of the tax burden.

Receiving the family home is the best value. Taxes on the appreciated value can be avoided if a new home is purchased within two years after the sale, or by taking advantage of the $125,000 capital gains exclusion for those over the age of 55.

## Closely Held Businesses

A major problem in many divorce settlements is determining value of a business. At issue is how much a non-working spouse indirectly has contributed to the success of the business. Receiving a percentage interest or income stream from such a business is probably not the best way to proceed. If that income dries up, any financial recovery will be difficult, if not impossible. A lump sum settlement, wherever possible, is usually best so the partners can go their separate ways.

## Professional Degrees

A new trend in divorce law is the claim that a professional degree or license can be marital property and its value divided. What is argued is that the non-student spouse deserves a share of future earnings because he or she has helped boost earnings by supporting the student while in school. This is not universal by any means, but the trend is certainly in this direction. In shorter marriages, the trend is to reimburse the working spouse for the cost of professional education of the other spouse.

## Insurance

Under federal law, health and life insurance coverage from a spouse's employer may be continued at group rates for up to 36 months after a divorce, regardless of which spouse pays for it. The law does not apply to those who are covered by another group plan, no matter how inadequate it might be.

## Retirement Benefits

Pension plans are likely to be the second largest asset and will be included in the divorce settlement. Federal law allows a spouse to receive a share of the benefits accrued during a marriage if the judge so decides.

Calculating the present value of future benefits is not easy, and most likely needs to be done by an actuary. Rather than wait for many years for a share of a company pension, a spouse might negotiate for a lump sum payment up front.

Under Social Security rules, a spouse may also receive some of the ex-spouse's benefits if the marriage lasted ten years. However, this will not be available until the former spouse retires or dies.

## When A Divorce is Planned

—Put away savings in a separate account, giving ready cash in case of emergency.

—Establish credit if not already present, apply for a credit card or have a friend co–sign for a small bank loan.

—Make an inventory of all assets, including investments, with account numbers, cars and home furnishings. Such information will be needed to determine a settlement. Have a bank verify the list of contents of any safety deposit box.

—Close out joint charge accounts, or if they are kept open, notify creditors that one spouse will no longer be responsible for the other spouse's purchases.

## During the Divorce Process

—Notify banks and brokerages where there are joint accounts of the intention to divorce. Ask that no transactions be carried out without the written approval of both spouses.

—Transfer all assets to an account where one spouse does not have unrestricted access.

## After Divorce is Final

—Rewrite a will to name an heir other than ex-spouse.

—Review health, life and disability insurance coverage. Change the beneficiary on all policies unless the settlement requires continued coverage. Replace any protection lost.

## Remarriage

In the event that a person wishes to remarry, a pre-marital agreement might be considered. This means that a legal document should be created on how the assets are divided. Much apprehension and potential problems may be avoided by such an agreement.

Divorce is tragic. Couples should do everything possible to find healing for a marriage, seeking the necessary help. But when divorce does take place, by a willingness to compromise, by keeping hostility at a minimum, financial costs can be kept much lower. And when financial costs are controlled, chances are that some of the other emotional costs will be controlled as well. Keeping divorce spending under control allows more resources and energy to be available for the challenge of starting over again.

# ORGANIZED RECORD KEEPING

Rewards which come from diligent and consistent record keeping cannot be overemphasized. With rather uncomplicated and minimal effort up front, much time and frustration can be prevented later on. In no more than one or two evenings, a complete system can be established, with only a few minutes required each week to keep it current.

Most of us have had the common experience of having to retrieve some kind of important document from the past, such as a tax statement, an insurance policy number, a money market or bank account number, or even the cost of a stock purchased long ago. When record keeping is slovenly, such a small task can become a significant chore.

Good organization of records is essential for good financial planning, and for the good mental health of each person. What exact shape that filing system will take is a matter of personal preference, but some basics should be considered.

Master File

Somewhere within easy reach of family and any financial advisors should be a very complete master file. Here is where people would turn if something would happen to us. Included in such a file should be the following:

—A list of assets and debts
—A copy of the will
—Information about safety deposit boxes, with keys
—Names and addresses of attorney, accountant, broker, insurance agent
—Financial institutions where accounts are held, together with the account numbers
—Birth and Marriage Certificates
—Funeral Information
—Death Benefits
—Veterans Benefits
—Purchase price of any assets acquired within the past three years

Active and Inactive File

Once a year the files should be pruned. Papers which need to be kept should be transferred from an active to an inactive file, and those which are no longer needed can be tossed. To be completely safe, most information for taxes should be kept up to six years.

Some files to be maintained:

—Bank file. Keep cancelled checks, monthly account statements, as well as deposit and withdrawal statements until they show up on the monthly account.

—Money Market. Monthly or quarterly statements should be kept as well as cancelled checks and records of deposits.

—Mutual Funds, CD's. Keep a separate file for each of these, at least until they are sold and the tax information is complete.

—Contributions. Gifts to the church should be recorded, as well as any expenses incurred as a volunteer. Papers necessary to document any gift of property are essential.

—Automobile file. Keep a separate file for each car, including title, bill of sale, warranties, maintenance record, receipts for expenses, license information, record of loans or lease information.

—Residence file. Keep all records of the purchase of the home, as well as those for improvements. Hold these indefinitely, they will be needed for tax purposes when the home is sold. Keep records of mortgage payments, real estate taxes, annual statements of interest and principal. Utility and phone bills can be discarded unless they are needed for business or charity.

—Employment information. Paycheck stubs may be kept, especially those for the final paycheck of the year, giving information for tax purposes. Keep W-2 forms, other benefits, or profit sharing documents. Record deductible travel, entertainment or gift expenses. A paid receipt is required for every business expense over $25.

—Pension information, together with IRA, Keogh or any other tax deferred savings.

—Insurance. Keep a separate file for each major category: life, health, car, home.

—Investments. A separate file should be established for each stock, bond, mutual fund or advisor that is used. Purchase and sales slips should be kept, as well as monthly or quarterly statements. Retain the cost basis in any investment, needed to prove any gain or loss.

—Medical. Keep medical history records here as well as any receipts for medical expenses.

—Other real estate. Complete records should be maintained for second homes, any land, or partnerships.

—Major purchases. Keep information about boats, trailers, motor homes, lawn equipment, as well as warranties.

—Tax information. Separate files for each year of tax returns, up to six years are important. For the most recent year, keep an extensive file of all pertinent information. At the time of tax preparation, cull all of the files for additional data and incorporate into the tax file.

—Education file. Record any college costs, private school information, continuing education for any member of the family, degrees earned and credit information.

<u>Where To Store Records</u>

A good solid metal *file cabinet* is the best place for important records. Make sure the space is expandable. Records will grow over the years, not diminish. Fire resistance is an essential ingredient of this file cabinet. If the rest of the home is destroyed, the records will still be intact.

A *safety deposit box* should be used for those documents which would be difficult to replace. Vehicle titles, stock and bond certificates, an inventory and photos of your household possessions should be in this safe place. Important legal papers such as trusts, real estate deeds and a list of insurance policies should also be there. The policies may be kept at home, they are easily replaced by the company if misplaced.

Do not keep a will or any other document needed at the time of death in the safety deposit box. Often the box is sealed, although each state has different statutes. Ask the bank what the respective policies are.

Instead, the will should be kept in a fire resistant place in the home, with a note in the master file about where it is located. A lawyer should also have a copy in case the original is lost, then it can be re-drawn.

Record keeping sounds mundane and often is relatively low on the priority list. But if it is established correctly in the first place, very little effort need be expended after that. Be reminded that the amount of frustration and hassle which can be saved for family members in a time of crisis can be immeasurable. Avoid problems, keep good records in a secure place in an organized way.